de book of Joseph

BOOKS BY PAMELA MORDECAI

Poetry
Journey Poem
de man: a performance poem
Certifiable
The True Blue of Islands
Subversive Sonnets
de book of Mary: a performance poem
Up Tropic
A Fierce Green Place: new and selected poems

Fiction
Pink Icing: stories
Red Jacket: a novel

For Children
Storypoems: A First Collection
Don't Ever Wake a Snake
Ezra's Goldfish and Other Storypoems
Rohan Goes to Big School
The Costume Party

de book of JOSEPH

A PERFORMANCE POEM

Pamela Mordecai

MAWENZI HOUSE

We acknowledge the support of the Canada Council for the Arts for our publishing program. We also acknowledge support from the Government of Ontario through the Ontario Arts Council, and the support of the Government of Canada through the Canada Book Fund.

Cover design by Pamela Mordecai and Sabrina Pignataro
Author photo credit: David Mordecai

Library and Archives Canada Cataloguing in Publication

Title: De book of Joseph : a performance poem / Pamela Mordecai.
Names: Mordecai, Pamela, author.
Description: Poem in Jamaican Creole.
Identifiers: Canadiana (print) 20220191549 | Canadiana (ebook) 20220191581 | ISBN 9781774150726
   (softcover) | ISBN 9781774150733 (EPUB) | ISBN 9781774150740 (PDF)
Classification: LCC PS8576.O6287 B66 2022 | DDC C811/.54—dc23

Printed and bound in Canada by Coach House Printing

Mawenzi House Publishers Ltd.
39 Woburn Avenue (B)
Toronto, Ontario M5M 1K5
Canada
www.mawenzihouse.com

Praise for Pamela Mordecai

Subversive Sonnets

"This is a remarkable book of sonnets which are subversive in wonderful ways."

—Elaine Savory, Emeritus Professor, The New School

"Like Pamela Mordecai's other work, *Subversive Sonnets* is clever, witty, insightful and linguistically acrobatic. Never one to shy away from difficult themes, Mordecai employs the sonnet form to sing more than 'little songs'. There is organ music here too as thematically she moves between the bottomless deeps and praise of heaven's wonders. A courageous, affirmative, and—yes—entertaining read. A wise, highly crafted and satisfying exploration of life deeply lived in all its infinite refractions and life as we'd like it to be."

—Olive Senior, author of *Dancing Lessons*

"*Subversive Sonnets* is an astonishing achievement. Beautifully gloved in the materiality of everyday things and not-always everyday places, these poems yet push the reader towards speculative realms of gold, where real places also become mind places and homes of deep feeling. Mordecai readily takes us from the finely personal to wider grief for North America's, the Caribbean's, and all our sins, from the saucily bawdy to political fury and horror at a New World turned bitterly, bitingly old, or from a joyous bounce to subsequent personal loss and collective agony that can become skin-crawlingly terrifying. These sonnets are the achievement of years of a poet's wisdom."

—Timothy J Reiss, Professor Emeritus of Comparative Literature, New York University

"*Subversive Sonnets* is sweet, acerbic, scintillating, and sassy. If you want to be right, you can't go wrong in reading these verses that modernize the sonnet, putting it in service of mischief, not only meditation. Mordecai has assembled a collection that is arrogant in its dazzle and provocative in its sizzle. Here's the real poetry, folks: thought given discipline and then set free to sing and/or singe."

—George Elliott Clarke

de book of Mary

"*de Book of Mary* is both a salute to [Jamaica's] colourful patois that [the poet] so loves and a fresh spin on age-old, Bible-based lore."

—*Tallawah Magazine*

"[T]his is an imaginative take on a familiar story."

—*Herizons*

"Mordecai re(claims) and re-centres the story of Maiden Mary, triumphantly transposing it from the word of men to the stories of women, and from High Church language to everyday speech. As did Derek Walcott before her, she performs the legacy of Caribbean creolization; a muscular hybrid which claims the right equally to the ancient forms of Greek theatre, the traditional practices of Judaism, and the beauty of Caribbean vernaculars and sensibilities. A lovely, chewy book."

—Nalo Hopkinson, author of *The Salt Roads*

"A rare and dazzling look at her world and ours by one of the most mysterious women of all time."
—Rachel Manley, author of *Drumblair: Memories of a Jamaican Childhood*

"*de book of Mary* is a perfect example of how powerful, striking stories will always, in every place and era, find exactly the right person to re-tell them. The poet Pamela Mordecai has found a new way with the Good News—*de book of Mary* is a page-turner—pure energy released through pure poetry."

—JonArno Lawson, author of *Sidewalk Flowers*

to

Martin Manley Mordecai
18 November 1942 — 19 February 2021

funny ting.

not keh-keh like a trickster.

just funny peculiar as Matthan would say.

talk truth. who would ever expect de likes of a small town
tekton to be telling dis tale? to be talking a story like dis?

is Matthan same one say if you live long enough you see some
peculiar tings.

and talk truth me did live long enough to see nuff peculiar
tings . . .

1: the goats and the wood

I

Ma say it take me two whole day to find my way out her belly.

"Ma! don't is you always say 'if you want good your nose have to run'?

"don't is you say 'long road draw sweat. short cut draw blood'?

"don't is better de long road and me reach in one piece?

"next ting me come quick and kill de two of we?

"next ting me alter destiny?

"mash up what can't never fix back?"

is not carpenter work i was born to. no sir. my pa Jacob and Matthan him father before and Eleazar before him go back and go back was people raise goat and sheep kind.

Uncle Reuben Pa one bredren is de tekton mongst us. is him ply de carpenter trade.

Gramps was ra'ah—a born tender of sheep and goat kind. like him navel string cut on de borning of kids de rearing dem shearing dem keeping dem safe.

seeing dem kosher to table as kashrut prescribe. as Leviticus and Deuteronomy state.

Uncle Reuben had a way to say "de shekels my friends is in two tings. food and frailty. dis fambili response for de two. all who work wid sheep and goat provide for de food. we dat work wood and stone response for de frailty. from life start till it done. cradle to ossuary."

when de desert come in and de grazing get sparse we let go
de sheep and keep on wid de goat for you know goat throat
tough. him will nyam brick and bramble and be none de
worse.

gramps say "feed a ram wid a rock and him grow never mind
and him put out him beard and him breed. feed a doe wid a
thorn she full out and carry her kid go one side set him down
when her kidding time come.

"just as faithful as showers and sun."

so we minding we goat making life and de life we was making
was good.

den de foot rot set in. in one moon we lose seven score goat.
like a piece of Pa die wid every ram doe likl kid dat drop dead.

i sure it was going kill Pa but is not him it kill.

is we Grandpa Matthan.

some did swear is a curse Jahweh send seeing as how we foot swell so we sandal can't fit. dem did cackle and hoot.

"monkey climb up too high—monkey backside expose!"

some say we did tink we was better dan dem so it well serve we right.

mark you is de same some come running for Gramps when goat kid get stuck in doe womb lock dem knee say no way dem ready to born.

"beg you tell de goat doctor we need him right now. we will pay."

and Gramps come and him pull out de baby goat-dem for no fee.

Gramps dead three week after de last ram give in.

dem best find a next goat midwife like how dis one gone.

me did miss Gramps for true. was a man full of jokes. was a man tell a story make your side burst wid laugh.

nuff time de story was bout sheep and goat.

him tell us de tale of two lamb. Hem and Haw. two twin bwoy.

when dem mother time come was a wicked wet night round de end of Adar. lightning flash. thunder roll. hill and gully quake de length and de breadth of Judea.

but Ma Sheep did ready.

Hem was on him way down well eager head first when a sinister class of lightning explode. Hem two ears retreat and him turn him head bleat "me going let you go first Haw. you lead and me follow."

so Haw slide around Hem on him way to de world when a hell clap of thunder rough up earth sea and sky. brisk like fresh breeze a-morning Haw shimmy back up into him mummy tummy.

"my bredren" Haw say "is not dat i ungrateful for your consideration but out of respect me tink you should go first."

wise men in Galilee say until today dose two lamb Hem and Haw still obliging each other.

none of dem don't yet reach Jah-Jah world.

Gramps slap him knee and him laugh can't stop.

6

not a sheep nor a goat nor a shekel did leave so it never make
sense to keep on. and me was a youth never reach sixteen
yet so me never did feel any way when Uncle Reuben take it
upon himself to learn me de carpenter trade.

i take my two long clumsy hand and two foot and repair to
him yard.

repair is de word for we do nuff repair. we mend stool bench
and table if dem lame no mind if is stone or is wood. now and
den we shore up a rafter dat hold up a roof. if we lucky we get
to throw up a lean-to for kitchen or porch.

and we make handle for plough and hoe.

de sweetest is coaxing a cradle from stone. is a job don't too
often come for dis not a big town and one cradle can serve a
whole fambili pikni after pikni.

so me watch and try learn what Uncle Reuben learn me and
me tell myself who beg can't choose.

and each day me wait on de wood . . .

7

for a shepherd de woodwork was hard.

true in time my heart learn to rejoice at de shape of a door
or de heft of a hoe or de carving atop a lintel but it never
compare to de ebb and de flow de ripple and swell of de side
of a doe as de goat pikni romp in her womb.

and me miss de small stones of goat dung and de smell of
goat piss and de blood of de doe in her time.

but mostly me miss de slithering out of de kids de stumble to
walk and to run and de joy when we find a lost one when we
follow de feeble *baa-baa* scour hill and cliff side till we fish it
from out a sly crack.

and de song as we walking it back.

8

was a long time before me discover de life of de wood.

it sweet my nose right from de first.

as de shavings curl up from de plane sliding true down de
grain of cedar or acacia or pine dem summon de earth and de
wide open sky and de growing of green.

all de same me work wood for more dan three year before
a shape sing down my arm connect wid de board make de
bloom of itself.

before me hearken as wood yield and reply to de hammer de
saw and de plane.

9

wood and me born as seed. grow like reed. die. go back to
dutty. me and it did take time to say howdy. meet and greet.
fuss and turn friend again.

maybe is why in de end we get on.

but me and rockstone was a next nother ting.

it resist from de start. i wrestle wid it. take stone axe and lick
it. drill it. cut it wid saw. mould wid mallet and pick.

fight to hew block to make floor and wall.

fight for even small tings. shape a basin a bowl.

it own way. it take it sweet time to concede. no goat nor ass
kind more wayward dan dat lime.

make me tink how we Israelite struggle just to make life. how
we joust wid de Roman downpressor for freedom and food.

how we dig out we life from de Babylon Roman quarry.

was de day me was cutting a crib for a babe.

Uncle Reuben last dawta Dina was making her first. de chile was to come at Pesach—de Passover festival. she and James her husband moving into dem own house soon-soon. Uncle Reuben done carve a table for dem a bench couple stool and a chest.

who know what make him take it into him head to fashion a chair dat can rock?

when him tell me me ask him "but for what Uncle Reuben? for what?"

him smile. "Joseph you tink Roman downpressor hatch havoc? dem is nothing compare to newborn!"

and him make it you know! was de first man to do it in all Galilee! shape a smooth arc of wood to join up de two foot on each side. shave and plane. match de curves and den plane dem again.

first time him sit in it him so please wid himself dat him push back too far make de ting pupalick.

me frighten so till for him is a big man and me hear someting crack when him drop! *bu-du-dup*!

i bend down to help him but him jump up same time laughing like a pikni.

"sit and swing in it Joe! don't you see me make a miraculous ting?"

in a town small like dis de tekton business tilt up and tilt
down like de new rocking chair. never mind everybody want
rocker Uncle Reuben can't meet de demand for wood scarce.

him had was to find a next work to keep head pon shoulder
and fill pikni belly.

so we turn to de sea.

now and den Uncle Reuben was use to help him friend
Jonah wid de fishening. Jonah was Pa friend too and a good
fisherman. is him teach me to swim when me small. now him
show me de ways of de sea and learn me from likl to big how
de fishening go.

me take to fishening right from de start. it sweet me to
bounce on de sea like me on donkey back when him running.
rise and fall wid each stride of de waves.

so we three on Lake Kinneret deep in de night throwing
net left and right wrestling water when wind wild it up in a
storm.

and a wish twist my tripe one of dem devilish night.

*to shear off de tangle up wool of my life. to card it and spin it—
make a fine woven ting. like de rockstone to have my own way.*

me was glad in my life.

den me turn seventeen. Pa say look for a wife.

Ma was sprightly and spry so me never know why him get it in him head me must get married. is not like Ma need help in de house.

true my bredren Eli dat come first did married long since gone to Hebron to join him wife fambili business.

Jonathan de last one did answer circumstance when him marry Suzanna one year gone. de two fambili-dem gree she best stay at her father yard for she was well sick wid de child and is two meyaldot her ma and grandma in dat house.

it leave me Ma and Pa but we three going on good. work eat sleep and play. pray three time a day Shaharith Minhah and Maariv.

but me tink Pa did fraid me would fall into coarse company. Roman soldier-dem was a vile lot. some of Israel youth did take to dem ruinous ways.

"if a man satisfy at him yard" Pa was helping Ma make up a fire one night "him not likely to run down de road and look woman . . . "

Ma kiss teeth. "Jacob you and me know plenty Jew leave dem good spouse a-yard and walk street to go find a next bed . . . "

"wife is one child leave wid we and me love him bad. me must do right by him. de bwoy need to lie down and rejoice."

13

like me say already dis not a big town.

my fambili screen from scarf down to sandal in synagogue market all down by lakeside where fish sell morning time.

but like spite is cousin from courtyard to corner. a maddening swarm of near blood.

still Ma have her ways when it come to dem tings.

"dis one town is not all Galilee!" she tell Pa. "just left it to me and de sistren. we going find a sweet girl what come from decent table. Joseph going married before cool-and-rain come."

no way not to trust Ma.

before dry time finish she arrive wid a name.

Deborah.

black hair wid nuff twist tell me some son of Ham interfere
in de line a long time aback. not a curl but it tease and play
catch wid de light and delight as it long down her back.

she was brown as a nut wid small breast and broad hip and
puss eye. lazy and impudent.

not pretty but velvet and sharp as new wine.

first time me see her she did look straight at me—no eye-to-
de-ground back of eyelid half-close and prim.

it don't reach my face but me feel my gut grin.

and me straightway give thanks to De-One-Dat-Run-Tings
for me know in my heart when de sistren and Ma was
scouring Galilee dem was walking wid Jah.

2: Debs and me

15

"she will make plenty sons." dat is Pa.

"you have writing to establish is sons she going bear?" dat is Ma.

"all right old woman. she will make nuff pikni. you satisfy now?"

"you could talk for yourself but you better don't call me old. old fowl can't mind nest. and furthermore Deborah not no milch cow set to churn out baby. it don't suit man to grind away woman body."

"is what ail you Milcah my love? like you rise wid wasp nest underneath your kethōneth!"

"de young woman will manage. she can weave keep house look after pikni. best of all she know her own mind. not going take no foolishness from dat son of yours."

"son of mine? is not your pikni too?"

"so you ready Miss Debs?"

on de day of nissuin Debs was a tzebi de loveliest doe in all Israel.

her ma take off de veil she live in since erusin—de day we betroth. Debs bat her eye like she come back from de blind. toss her head like jackass when you loosen de noose of a rope from him neck.

when me fancy dat hair in my nose dem plum breast in my chest dat slim waist in my arms my blood heat up and sing like hot olive oil. me glad me was helping Reuben wid de fishening so de dark of my skin maybe hide de flush and keep it from show.

six month gone Jacob pay de mohar de bride price to Debs pa. now me come wid my friend-dem and folks to take Debs to live in my father house.

is a brazen blue day. we blow de shofar on de way so Debs and her people can know we coming. de bredren carry nebel and tonbak and timbrel to make a sweet noise as we walking Debs home.

me gazing at Debs. Debs gazing at me. me look to her ma for my permit. she raise eyebrow screw up mouth point her chin wid inquiry at Debs.

"yes Ma. me ready."

Debs climb on de litter and we start de journey.

me know wid dis woman me going weave a fine ting.

me inspect Debs belly like me was use to watch doe as dem brewing goat kid. every day a next move a next shape a next tune.

de first day him kick me certain me feel it before Debs see her middle grow into a mount wid a slow wriggling ridge.

Debs look down wid her jaw in her neck.

me don't dare laugh out but me make up my mind me could run likl joke.

"Debs . . ." me say "it look like de bwoy find him foot!"

me know de baby for a bwoy from de start and same so him did know himself as him open him jaw and bawl out. we call him Ezekiel for my best pasero sake of de lopsided mouth.

18

Debs get pregnant again but she lose de girl baby. so like
Father Abraham me bargain wid God.

"Jah you can take de house de business my foot or my hand
but beg you ease up on my woman."

time pass and me plant a next seed and dis time it grow and
bear fruit we pluck. we name him Aaron for Debs pa.

me rejoice for me tink Jah relent but is him did laugh last.

de next pikni so strong in de womb him thump like him
punching right through Debs belly.

but Jah take we for sport. land we wid a *boof*. never mind de
girl chile leave Debs womb soft and warm her spirit was gone.

she was stiff in no time.

stone cold dead.

Zeke and Aaron strive. dem firm on dem foot and can feed dem own self. know to pee and to poo. can sit quiet and listen to story and song. can tell dem own story. sing dem own song too.

me take dem to de workshop to witness de work. learn dem to reckon wid measuring reed and leveling line.

me and Debs make a plan. we waylay de rabbi and ask him what age pikni can start school. we tell rabbi what tings dem can do.

rabbi gree so we send Zeke and Aaron to de pikni school. dem learn de Shema in de old Hebrew Tongue. de Ten Sayings.

mezonot—de blessing on bread.

dem take turns when we eat. Debs love hear dem recite.

"Blessed are you Adonai De-One-Dat-Run-Tings who cause bread to come forth from de earth."

till now Debs breed and she bear and for each pikni dat live de next baby die. it try me so sore me did keep from her bed but she don't take to she one on de mat.

"Joe me never married to lie down wid no cat! me miss de lovin."

being Debs dat was dat.

and so it go on. de next baby born strong. one girl we call Judith.

pikni shoot through we life like a star . . .

de likl girl Judith grow like a wild creature. dat chile was my heart but she bad like a sore. never hear a command de first time. fraid no person nor ting. climb a wall hillside tree like Sheba monkey. race like cheetah and cunning like fox.

from de start me and Debs fuss bout dat girl pikni.

"who going married to her? so saucy and own way!"

"but after you wasn't no meek-as-lamb bride. who de chile could take after but you same one Debs? she don't have no example but you."

"you see my dying trial! me? saucy? own way? husband Joe? what a liar you be!"

Debs was dead set on sending Judith to pikni school.

me know dat can't work so me strike a deal wid her. she and me gree as Zeke come home him will learn Judith de tings de rabbi learn him.

me give it to Zeke how him manage him unruly sister. Aaron love invent tunes so Zeke ask him to make up a song wid numbers to help her recall.

Zeke write dem big-big in dutty wid a stick.

dem save date and fig to give her when she sing de song right or say couple line from de Shema.

and me and Debs watch as de pikni dem grow.

me see de wheel spin. see de thread emerging. see a fine ting weaving.

Debs belly grow a next time but de bwoy chile slip away.

me get well wrathed so me address Jah again.

"Elohim you romp rough. what me or my wife do to you? why you capture we offspring like wild dog grab gazelle?"

i double my two fist and shake dem at him.

Debs frighten for so. "Joseph you can't address Jahweh in dat reckless fashion. mind you make him worse vex!" and she beat her right fist on her breast tabering.

"after Jah-Jah is not any small time despot. King of Kings Lord of Lords have better tings to do dan to hold feeble protest gainst me and gainst you!"

24

look like Jah heed my cry.

de next time after a likl girl born and we call her Sarah.

me lie flat on my face and give thanks to Elohim for him
never grudge me neither pain neither plea.

a gentle sweet chile from she born . . .

Debs bad luck wid borning baby never change. when she lose a next one after Sarah me beg her hold up likl bit.

"hold up? but Joe is not me to hold *up*. is you or is me doing de holding down here?"

"i do not recall ever holding you down Debs. seem to me we did gree on any holding betwixt you and me."

"talk truth me love have you in my belly Joe." and she laugh like water jumping down de Sa'ar Falls.

she could be bad-behave when she choose my Debbie!

"but Joseph my spouse must i now understand you telling me you desire a next plan?"

"i am telling you Debs your body don't make from rockstone. me love loving you more dan life but me rather not kill you wid making baby."

"Joe me tell you nuff time me rather dead fat wid a baby dan live wid a man me can't sweet wid loving."

and Debs push me down flat.

de next baby start come sudden down in de night before de set time.

Debs tie up like twine in a ball from de pain.

me frighten send Zeke to go get Miss Rachel from next door. me tell him fetch de midwife down de hill after dat.

me wait and me wait and can't see not a soul.

sweat cover Debs body. her teeth hard in her lip till blood draw. den she heave and her knee bruck apart and de baby slide out after Debs push two time.

a beautiful babe wid a head full of hair.

cold and limp. not a breath. and is me one and Debs.

Debs say "Joe don't mind me. me can manage. tend to de baby."

de pikni cold like winter rain. lip and finger mist blue.

me quick burn my knife in de flame of de lamp. wipe wid wine. cut de cord. dip a cloth in warm oil. clean off de baby.

den me grab one of Debs simlāh and wrap de chile tight. curl her into my chest.

she still cold.

me suck out her nose. take my finger and open her mouth. suck de slime from dere too.

lip and finger still blue.

me cover her nose and her mouth wid my mouth and puff air in her chest. one time den a next and a next and a next. me squeeze de small chest gentle in gentle in. den me do de whole process again.

and at last she draw breath.

me laugh loud me so glad. turn and give Debs de chile.

de baby on her breast but Debs face don't look good. me take de afterbirth and set it one side. me know blood is to come but de red bubbling out Debs belly come like a fountain.

same time Zeke arrive wid Miss Rachel and Miss Dor de meyaldot.

poor fellow him so weary him eye shutting down. me pat him on him shoulder.

"son you must be well tired. thanks for bringing Miss Rachel and Miss Dor. now go catch some sleep."

de two woman shoo me outside to fetch water.

"make a fire in de courtyard. heat it till it well hot. we will need it in time."

me wait and me watch till de fire decay and my chin touch
my chest.

when morning light me go down to de shop like me custom
to do. at about de third hour Zeke and Aaron come to collect
me behind two broad smile.

"come Pa Joe. Ma say time to break fast."

me careful to put down de chisel. go wid dem to de cistern.
we all wash we hand good go inside to see Debs setting food
on de table. Judith and Sarah paste to her kethōneth gazing
on de new baby bright in her hand.

we sit down. me open my mouth to pray over de bread.

a voice pry my eye open. bring me into de day.

"we well sorry Maas Joe. Miss Deborah gone and she take de
baby."

rake my heart when me tink how Debs die bringing we last pikni den like crosses de baby die too.

i send my mind back to my shepherding days.

fire water sharp knife and a clean stretch of cloth or animal skin and a pan of water. make no difference de animal kind. dem come into de world de same way.

and me have so much practice me can do it now wid a rag tie to blind my two eye.

me know me did do what de baby did need.

but if midwife was dere from de start maybe Debs and de chile wouldn't dead.

den me hear her clear-clear.

"not so Joe. was my time. was her time."

31

Debs and me share life near to seventeen year and each year
it out-pass de last one. we wake work and worry. fight and
make up.

make and bury baby.

it all done in de split of a meagre minute. so breeze drop and
flame die so Debs flicker away.

me wail for de short perfect weave of we life.

3: two little lambs

praise Jah for de two lamb. dem keep me on my foot apron tie
round my waist eye fix on fowl nest ear out for fisherman wid
him fresh morning catch.

nose tune so de stink of stale clothes don't send news down
de road.

is dem keep me going on never mind my head drunk wid de
wine Debs don't pour my belly bawl out for her food . . .

night time was de worst. last ting me and Debs do as we float
de Shema through de window to heaven is number de stars.
now every creature dat crawl hear de word-dem drop pon de
ground like stone round Debs ossuary.

me's a man coax goat kid and lamb kid to hold on never mind
de doe dead for each life is a promise each bleat a new hymn
to Elohim.

not so different minding dose girls.

mark you me still do de tekton work. Zeke and Aaron work
wid me dese days so me leave de two girl pikni next door wid
Miss Rachel when need call we to a next yard.

me barter repair a stool here a bench dere for her time.

when dem visit de shop de two likl girl play wid one-two
piece of wood. pile up three-four stone. learn to number de
wood and de stone wid help from dem bredren.

learn to tell different wood by de smell.

learn to use nail and hammer. put dem back in dem place.

time she turn eight Miss Judith could cipher like long head
tax collector and likl Miss Sarah her eye and her finger gauge
mortise and tenon good as carpenter reed.

what to do wid de bwoy-dem like how dem turn man? me no
like dem pon street. every corner you bend Roman soldier-
dem grinning dem wicked teet. plus downpression breed
desperation. dese days it seem like every last soul in Judea vex
at de same time.

was a ting ride my mind day in and day out. good enough
dat dem under my eye working wid me in de shop. but we
have tekton sufficient in dis likl town and if Jah-Jah give dem
talent is use dem must use it.

praise be to El Deah Him-Dat-Know-Everyting! straight out
of de depths of de quarry eternal me dig up a course for de
two bwoy to take.

Zeke love teach. maybe sake of de fact we did set him to learn
Judith what him glean at pikni school.

and Aaron love music. him make tune and play song de whole
livelong day.

me talk to de rabbi and him say okay. him could do wid de
four extra hand. now come morning time Zeke trod up de
slope wid a fatherly frown and Aaron tra-la-la back of him to
help teach Jah pikni.

35

Debs spirit departed suck joy from my soul. leave me weightless and chaff.

still de girl pikni-dem puncture hole in my pain.

"Pa Sarah fall down! scrape her knee!"

"Pa Judith put de puss in de tree. can't make him come down."

dat girl Judith quick wid her head and her lip. what a pikni give talk! what a chile wid a navel string cut pon argument! plus she can't stay one place. if me talking to her and turn way likl bit time me turn back to finish she gone.

and like how Debs travel and me have work to get through . . .

me pray every day. Jah-Jah what me must do?

is Hannah my mother big sister first dawta take it pon herself. come down here to dis house on Preparation Day in Nissan. station herself like centurion by we front porch and stand watching Judith and Sarah rock and roll round de yard wid Zana from next door.

massa sun gather up him simlāh say goodbye take him leave. same time Miss Rachel come out de next house. she wave and call out. shoo de three girl inside. shout to me.

"de likl ones coming just now."

Hannah turn to me. "Joseph you and me have to talk."

well Miss Hannah and me never have no palaver before. plus she and my Debs never into no chit-chat.

now it seem we need conversation.

me skin teeth. "but cuz" me declare "you and me—don't we talk all de time?" playing fool to catch wise Debs would say.

"dis is serious Joe. not no laughing matter. put de knife down and sit."

must be serious in truth for is orders now giving. me a man careful how me issue pronouncement so me don't rightly take to nobody pronouncing on me. still me tired. too tired to bring argument. me loose my apron. hang it pon de peg.

"see" she point to de table inside "me bring some new bread Miss Annie bake. say me must leave wid you and de girls for Shabbat."

me draw water and bring. some for she some for me. take my

time and lie back in Reuben rocking chair.

"very kind of you to bring de bread" i tell her. "i will make
sure to tell Miss Annie nuff thanks."

and i sip.

"now what bout dis serious business?"

"Rivka is a big woman. she older than you. well ripe past de time for bearing pikni. dat will suit you. four pikni is plenty enough. she have her own house couple pasture for sheep couple acre for grain and a small olive orchard to boot. mother dead father dead and she never married so she have no pikni."

"make she never married? is not a good sign."

"de parents was sick so she refuse all around and she take care of dem till dem dead."

"she don't have no sistren nor bredren?"

"not a one. you recall de bad fever when you and me small? it take all six but she."

"me well sorry to hear."

"she not young neither pretty" my cuz pressing on "and talk truth when she ready she can frown up her face."

how me going like frown-up face? Debs was a honeycomb.

"but seeing as how is she one and she have house and land your well and her well not going never run dry. and come right down to it way inside is a sweet tranquil soul."

but how far inside till me reach to de sweetness and calm?

Hannah say de day after Shabbat she going bring Rivka come to meet me and de two bwoy and de two girl pikni.

first day after Shabbat sun fry egg. was past de sixth hour
when Aaron and Zeke stop bruck stone and stumble inside.
it so hot it red up de brown in de bwoy-dem skin. dem parch
till dem empty one whole water jug. each.

me take one look askance on de bright in de yard and me say
"you two best stay inside till de new day start."

so dem pon de step watching de three girl pikni chase fowl in
de next yard when Cousin Hannah and Miss Rivka reach to
we gate.

"evening sistren" me say. "welcome into de dwelling of a
proud descendant of de tribe of David."

is not boast me boasting but my line go far back through my
father him father and him father before. it go all de way up to
de warrior David sweet warbler in front de altar of Jah.

Rivka touch de mezuzah step inside. Cousin Hannah nod
prim like Rivka is her dawta. Rivka don't answer me but me
see her two eye gather dust from de corner and mud off de
floor.

"me would glad if you meet my two son Miss Rivka. dis is
Aaron de youngest and de long one over dere is Ezekiel my
first. dem will see to your comfort while me gather de girls."

de bwoy-dem stand to greet her as me slip cross de yard
and me see Rivka head make two bounce. her lip-dem don't
twitch. her face flat like matzah.

Hannah mouth corner lift and subside.

me still watching dem as me push Miss Rachel gate.

Hannah put her plump bottom pon de usual bench. Zeke
invite her companion to sit. bring cushion for her comfort.
Aaron bring a next one fat and full for her foot. she sit down.
settle straight like a plumb line. fold two hand in her lap.

Aaron go and come back wid de best water jug and a cup and
him pour. Rivka nod and she drink and she set de cup down.

not a sound. not a smile. not a sliver of sweet.

as me step pon Miss Rachel porch me see de two youth pull
one side and draw back in demself.

me say tanks to Miss Rachel for minding de girls. den me
quick herd Judith and Sarah out de door,

as me hustle back cross de courtyard me check to see if de clothes-dem set good round de two pikni neck.

me check dat hair draw back tidy. me make sure de four hand and two face not too full of dutty.

me mouth screw when me spot a rip in front Sarah kethōneth.

"is not she do it Pa. is Zana push her down make it tear!"

"not going put out de sun my dawta. don't fret. just member your manners. you too Miss Sarah. promise me?"

"yes Papa."

"yes Papa."

"come make we greet Miss Rivka Cousin Hannah good friend . . ."

me encourage dem up de three sulking stairs to where Hannah sitting wid de guest dipping bread in humus sipping juice from de sweet-orange grove up de road.

my last dawta is a soulful pikni. she take one look at Rivka.

El Shaddai what coming now? beg you make her don't cry.

me watch ready for what only Jah-Jah know . . .

Sarah scramble up beside Rivka. look up in her face. smile like a wood shaving curl from de plane .

"my name is Sarah. what dem does call you please?"

if me never did see it me wouldn't believe. me not no desert prophet but Sarah smile change Rivka like rain change tough dutty.

next ting me know is pure laughing and talk. Rivka give de two girl pikni joke. teach dem riddle. she all sing wid dem.

she get up and urge Hannah when Sarah insist. Zeke and Aaron and me watch incredulous as dem dance in a ring like four likl girls stead of two.

next day Hannah arrive well please wid herself.

"you see how Rivka and de two girl pikni get on? Deborah would be glad to know de girls have a mother to mind dem. you can't say no Joseph!"

"beg pardon Hannah but me's a plain talking man. is not Judith and Sarah nor Debs—Jah bless her—going lie down come night time wid Rivka."

"i have news for you cuz. you not shocking me . . . "

"so you get my meaning."

"me leave it wid you Joe. she done say she like you and de four pikni. she tink you and she would have a good life."

"it going have to wait till me beg Jah advice. wife not no easy ting."

"better don't say it twice lest you make Deborah vex."

"just go to show you never know Deborah good. she de first to agree."

"well talk when you ready."

"i will talk in Jah time. till den no bother harass me. i's a man approach tings slow and easy."

me hear her mumble as she make her goodbye. "bet Miss Debs did like dat."

me don't tink of myself as a prayerful man but me consult
Jah-Jah bout big matters in my life. any time me did fear for
Debs sake of baby business me jump on de shofar and send
him a shout.

Zeke say is de two likl girls she going mind and she and dem
get on like backside and bench.

*de girl pikni romp good wid Rivka is true. but is not dem beside
her day in and day out.*

"you could talk to de new rabbi Pa. him reach three day gone.
a youngish fellow but dem say him well smart."

trust Aaron to have news. when dat bwoy have free time him
either up de synagogue overlooking de runnings or down in
de market scrutinizing business.

him wise all dc same. you can learn plenty tings if de street is
your friend.

*but how old man like me must seek counsel from youth? still
according to Ketuvim Yahweh ordain strength out of de mouth of
infants and of babes . . .*

me decide to confer wid de new rabbi when me done work
next day.

de day was just turning sun stirring after him afternoon sleep eye blinking open but only to reckon him soon to be snoring again when me leave from my yard on de way to de synagogue top of de hill.

me wrangling de slope wid my staff when me buck up Nathan. him younger dan me but a widower still. first time when we was married him did live couple yard down de road from de fambili house.

"howdy Joseph. glad to see you! how you do? how de youth?"

"all hearty Nathan. praise Jah-Jah. how you going yourself? de pikni?"

"all good till now bredren. Jehovah be praised. me take it you heading for de synagogue?"

"yes is dere me going."

"and you carrying your stick!" him have a shy smile as him brandish him staff. "see me carrying mine!"

Nathan puzzle me. so him walk wid him stick. so me walk wid my own. what stick have to do wid de price of new wine?

him have de advantage of me if is some kind of joke.

"talk truth Nathan me not sure what you trying to say. me custom to walk everywhere wid dis crook from my shepherding days."

"ah my friend! you don't know? de new rabbi summon all de widower-dem. say we must come up to synagogue today and make sure we come wid we staff. me don't know if is fight we going fight or light we going light a big fire wid we widower stick!"

de laugh him did laugh vanish quick.

man slog up mountain but him bounce him way down
twinkle swift like a stream. is a usual ting.

dat evening me drag my two foot straggle back to my yard.

me not please wid de rabbi. young fellow look down pon bout
twenty Israelite some old till dem back bend like cashew and
give we instruction.

"go on home. get ready to journey to Jerusalem before Jah
light de sky tomorrow."

and further to dat we best make sure bring food and water for
three day. plus we staff.

rabbi tink say bread climb down out tree and run jump
pon table? him tink say de flesh of a lamb or a fish arrive
in de mouth of some bird flapping in pon him wing out de
heavenly blue?

him don't know Torah say we nyam bread by de sweat of we
brow?

and all like me . . . de two bwoy can mind demself but what
me to do bout de two girl pikni?

sun must be fry de brain of de new rabbi!

Roman say de gods use we for sport.

all who know Jah-Jah know him love play games but Elohim don't take we make joke. is true we is clay in him hand and is true him do as him please.

so tings work de best way when what please El Shaddai please you and me too.

best endeavour to do what Ten Sayings prescribe. best to praise and give thanks and surrender all tings to his mercy and gracious provision.

same so me strive to live all my life.

top de mount pon dat sweet green afternoon Jehovah set him hand down upon me tired pa of two youth and two likl girl pikni.

change my life after dat to a tale mighty strange.

4: Mary of Sepphoris

is two way to Jerusalem. one journey draw sweat. down de
hill cross de Plains of Esdraelon up Samaria heights south to
Jerusalem by de way de patriarch-dem Abraham and Isaac
and Jacob did walk.

de next longer route sidle east cross de Valley Jezreel den ease
south by de Jordan to turn hard by Jericho for a near straight
up climb back west to de holy city.

me surprise how de young rabbi easy wid himself and wid we.

when we gather at day clean him stand we in line every man
staff in hand bag of vittles and water-skin sling round him
neck. rabbi check we each one from toe to head top. count
we off as we pass de last house.

we go a short way and den him halt we and lead we in de
Traveller's Prayer.

"Jahweh our God and God of our ancestors we asking you
please to lead we towards peace. direct our foot so we stride
towards peace. make we reach where we going being life and
gladness and peace. keep we safe from de hand of de enemy
from tief and wild beast and from all breed of ambusher
assembling to assault we. beg you hear what we asking for
you is de Lord who listen to prayers."

den him lead a force march cross Samaria so in three day we
reach Jerusalem.

is not we alone reach. come morning four score man stand
up stink pon de temple porch staff in hand eyeball roaming
de gloam.

not a soul know de runnings. contention rise and fall like
wave surge and subside cruise to shore crash de rocks worry-
worry de sand like puss wid mus-mus.

man step from Court of Israel into Court of de Priests in a
stumbling horde. nuff clatter and bounce and "look where
you going!" and kiss teeth and "cho!"

high priest take him good time make all of dem wait.

when him stride from inside is not him one walking. back
of him to one side betwixt two temple crone is one girl chile
only just turn woman.

any shepherd can tell when a doe see first blood and is
shepherd me was at de start.

de old woman-dem walk each wid one hand pon her
shoulder

high priest stop and dem three stop same time.

de girl gaze pon one crone and de crone drop her hand. den
she eye de next one and she drop her hand too.

den she raise up her chin and she take in de crowd.

is a brown simple girl.

two dark eye rattle over de muddle of man. see each one wid
dem stick. rake dem through like a comb scour hair looking
lice.

me can tell dis young miss neither stupid nor idle nor have
time to waste.

me smile. me tink Debs would glad to behold a next woman
who know her own mind.

all de same like me say. a brown simple girl.

high priest wait till de widower-dem shut dem mouth.

"men of Israel behold Mary dawta of Maas Joachim and him good wife Miss Ann of de town of Sepphoris. dem did bring dem one dawta to dis holy place when she was three year old and leave her to serve Jehovah Most High.

"she serving Elohim from dat day to dis.

"but we know in Ketuvim Qohelet instruct dere is a time for everyting. a time to born and a time to die. a time to plant and a time to uproot. now is time for de dawtas of Israel dwelling in dis holy place and grown into woman to return to dem yard to married and raise up pikni.

"men of Israel when Mary hear is time to go home she say no she do not plan to stir. she insist on de promise her ma and pa make when dem vow her in service to Jah. and she further declare she her own self did promise her body and life to Jehovah.

"say no way she can don't keep her word.

"only one ting to do as high priest. i fall on my face in de Holy of Holies and beg El Shaddai for counsel.

"and behold in reply a voice sound through Court of de Priests and Court of Israel and Court of Woman. it say every last widower in de land must bring dem staff to de temple and lay pon de altar. de Spirit of Wisdom will choose one wid a sign. whomsoever dat branch belong to is de spouse for Mary.

"so i send out de word to all Galilee and Judea.

"widowers of Israel forward up as Elohim instruct and rest all de staff dem pon de altar of Jah."

is Matthan did teach me to discern twixt sign and
superstition.

him say if you studying sheep see dem clump up together
it probably mean look out for bad weather. dat's a forecast.
prediction. a natural ting.

him say you stupid if you tink a butterfly lit on your hand
mean nuff shekel or a black dog arrive in your path mean bad
luck.

by dat token what high priest now saying sound suspect to
me. de Spirit of Wisdom going give a clear sign? what kind of
clear sign? and how we to know?

den i member Tobias how him drive way de demon by
burning fish heart and fish liver as cording to how Azariah
instruct. Azariah was Angel Raphael in de guise of a man!

i pick up my staff join de line. rest it down. de staff-dem
stretch out all de way cross de altar from ebony black to de
white bleach of pine.

El Deah how me ever going know which branch belong to me?

man neck bend twist round swing right swing left eye peel
for omen but nary a stir on de ground in de air in de near or
de far in Court of Israel or Court of de Priests or de porch in
front de Holy Place.

den quick like a man explode in him joy one dove white as
light from nowhere come to rest on a rod as it burst into
bloom wid a trove of gold flowers.

silence drop like de lull in de eye of a storm.

how now to tell is who own de staff?

well de stick no get up find it way though de air to de hand of
de tekton from Nazareth town who of course is myself?

my jaw open close open close open close like jackass wid him
mouth in a hamper of straw.

gilt blossom-dem trembling leaves twinkled wid dewdrop de
dove like a song drifting softer and high in de sky.

a glorious ting but not of my making.

high priest don't waste no time.

pack my wife-to-be off to Sepphoris to her father house like
scapegoat to de desert.

not a hard ting to do for she have likl more dan de clothes
pon her willowy back. a blue shawl dat slide to a plump wide
backside a gift for bearing pikni—

is what i get myself into now?

de miracle story of de staff dat bear flowers and de dove dat
come clean out de air fly de length and de breadth of Judea
and Galilee. knock pon people mouth like disease.

how folks idle so? don't have nothing to do wid dem time?

dis Nazareth not a nice town. send blessing downhill and
time it reach bottom it turn into curse. susu take de tale twist
to nuff nastiness.

so me and Mary betroth on tiptoe.

no point adding breath to malevolent flame.

not to say de bride shy for is mettle me see when she smile
through de veil she must wear till de day we properly tie and
she leave her pa house and come to my yard.

me could tell she run deep like proverb declare of soft river.

Miss Ann warn me she own-way sometimes and me member
she did tell de high priest she not leaving de temple. none of
dat bother me. dis long time me living wid spunky in Debs . . .

but me know dat not fair.

Debs gone. Mary here.

de two girls still learning dem lesson.

is mostly Zeke teach dem. him did have a way wid Judith
from de start and where she lead Sarah bounded to follow.

Aaron play de timbrel and learn dem song and dance.

sometimes me laugh out as de four of dem prance. dem
remind me of Debs as dem swoop and dem leap like fish dat
can fly or bird dat can swim.

now not by my choosing but Jahweh decree a next woman
coming to run tings in dis place.

me feel Debs squeeze my hand. hear her say "is okay. is okay."

it prey on my mind dat Mary and Aaron is one age and
Ezekiel a full three year older dan she. true nuff widower
have bwoy pikni as old as dem second sometime dem third
wife. me would maybe not worry in a next town but in dis
Nazareth too much people bad mind.

Jah-Jah save me!

is two brother me have. both of dem in Judea. Eli come before
me. him have a business and live close to Hebron. Jonathan
de youngest keep a inn in Bethlehem.

Eli run a shop make shofar and timbrel and drum and de like.
from long time me know Eli not please wid him wife for is
only four dawta him have. me don't know how him figure is
him wife response!

in de midst of my worries me hear from Eli to say him would
glad for help in de shop.

me and Zeke and Aaron consult and decide dem will go to
Judea and help out Eli. Aaron full of excitement for him
expect him going meet musician and songwriter like him.

as for Zeke if is teacher him yearning to be Hebron is a most
ancient and learned city. him can train in dat trade give a
hand in de synagogue and practise right dere in de pikni
school.

hard to be in dis yard widout Aaron and Zeke.

de two girl pikni miss dem. miss de music and dance. even miss de learning. me hear Judith recite Maariv de evening prayer and Sarah try say it as she lead.

my hand on my head tinking to maybe married soon. like how me is a widower Mary and me don't have to wait out de whole year. when me sigh and look up who bless my eye but Rivka and Hannah stand up at de gate.

talk bout surprise!

me greet dem bid dem come inside and sit down. offer water to drink and mish-mish to nyam. ask after kin all de time wondering . . .

Hannah chewing not talking but she have a look like she well satisfy wid herself. Rivka face not so stiff and her mouth corner mild.

when Hannah done she lick her mouth and talk.

"we come wid good news Joe. member Nathan dat did live down de road from you and Deborah? him and Rivka betroth. she find a good man."

if is word Hannah throwing she welcome to throw. me not out to catch nothing. me glad for Rivka and me wish she and Nathan a long life wid nuff blessing.

she plenty older dan him but dat don't signify. it could be a good ting. Rivka look like she could need plenty husbanding.

like me say every day we tink bout de two bwoy but better
dem be where dem is.

Mary still at her father yard in Sepphoris. me check her de
first day every week when work at de stadium done. Miss Ann
don't take no when she and Maas Joachim and my betrothed
sit down to eat.

me tell her my supper expect me at my yard.

"den it will feed de mouth of some next hungry body!"

and de four of we laugh.

one day Mary look different. me love how her skin all de time
smooth and shine but now it alight not by candle nor fire but
like sun very self flaring from inside.

her eye soft like a secret.

hard to speak of to jostle weak words to say.

is Mary self tell me.

she was praying one morning bout de sixth hour and a
supersize angel just splash down same time bright like sun
black like night. she well fraid so she put her hand over
her eye but him tell her don't frighten. say him come from
De-One-Dat-Run-Tings to put question to her.

see me here well confuse for dat is plenty news! but seem best
to begin at de last.

"what kind of question?"

she say Jah send Angel Gabriel to ask if she will agree to have
him baby.

me say "hold down Mary. tell me one more time?"

so she say de same ting a next time word by word.

"Mary is joke you running wid me?"

"Joseph me serious as any shofet sit down in a trial to judge."

not every shepherd is a peaceable man but we don't rightly
thrive on commotion. it don't comfort de flock reassure de
just-born neither meld wid de quiet of empty hillside nor
cave dat yawn safe in de wrath of a storm.

true de tekton trade me ply dese last years is a next
dispensation for de hammer can rake up a ruckus and de saw
plane and chisel is rhythm or riot as cording to mood.

still is shepherding start me out when me was small and is it
set my temper. all who know me know peace as my bread and
calm as my wine. so no mind de noise of my nowadays trade
my spirit serene like any lamb sucking on him mother teat.

but Mary story start a rage in my soul unbeknownst before
dat time and since. me boil and me boil as me tink to
myself . . .

girl no more dan pikni and take big smadi for jackass!

me feel my hand rise de same way it stir to clap a rude pikni.
me had was to bolster myself in de door squeeze my two
palm hard gainst de doorpost and struggle to focus my brain.

me close my two eye. draw couple long breath. pull one
thought den a next like maggot from a wound.

is one hell of a story. me must give her dat. and she tell me
herself. respect for dat too. she me and her pa and ma know
is only one way out of dis if me turn my back left her. anyhow
it get out man going stone her to death in de entry way of dis
house.

me vex bad but me member a saying my pa used to say.

"do not speak in anger nor act when your blood hot. hurry
slow to conclusion no matter what."

and dis girl fill my eye and me take to her spunk de fling of
her head and her shoulder and hip.

me fasten my lip. open my two eye and look on her good. she
stand up same place but she now have a cup she offer to me.
i can see de tummy only need few more Shabbat and de news
will reach all Galilee.

i shake my head no to de drink. step through de door and
set off down de hill. good manners can stay on de shelf till
tomorrow.

when i turn back and look she still stand up holding de cup.

good ting is a long walk from dem house to my house. good
ting is near night for me talk to myself de whole way.

just as well dark conceal de mad muttering.

me don't figure Mary for a liar or a fool and she tell her story
wid her eye stick to mine constant as de dew dat sustain we
through dry time.

no eyelash don't flap nor no finger don't tap. no heel twist.
she rocksteady.

but de fact of de matter cash bill and receipt is she making
baby.

so is me must decide to condemn my betrothed to a death by
stoning and is me must determine de course if me spare her
from dat.

*is me have to weave wid de worst warp and woof of de wickedest
thread. like spite Jah-Jah now shift de shuttle back into my hand.*

when me reach home de two girl pikni fast asleep. Miss Rachel she rise when she see me come in. disappear as discreet as duppy.

me pour from de water jug and me drink deep. me did well want de water Mary offer me but me worse want her know say me mad like mad ram.

Jehovah de whole ting don't make no sense to me.

first one big procession of widower-man stoke de fire of de hill wid dem staff. gallop three day through dread mountain to Jerusalem. den de black brown white yellow and tawny array of stave upon stave on de altar in front de Holy of Holies.

den de blossom by conjure and de dove from nowhere.

and as sudden surprise dis simple brown girl a gift from Jehovah me figure to settle my life. to take for my wife when time come.

maybe weave a next wondrous ting.

was too soon for my heart but my spirit did take to her right from de start. now she insprignant and is not my pikni and a man have him pride.

plus is my woman now to do wid as i please.

though eye for a eye is what Torah command me can't say is a way me admire. me don't have no patience wid stoning a dog much less a woman. so is one ting to do. send her far from disgrace from de craven blood lust in dis cruel place.

me sigh as me sink to my mat. check de sky.

hear Debs as me sight de evening star.

me sleep and me dream. and is must angel time for is angel me dream. a big one. brown like bronze. hair like wool. shine like sun.

summon me by my name.

"Joseph hear a message from De-One-Dat-Run-Tings. son of David you don't have to fraid to take Mary unto you as your wife for is Jah Spirit give her de baby."

and him go on and say exactly what Mary did say.

"she going bear a bwoy chile. you must call him Yeshua for him going save Israel from dem sins."

if is dat him coming for de poor pikni have a sore time ahead.

me nod. "yes angel sir. me well understand."

me's a man lose no time. by nightfall next day me and Mary married and her bag and baggage was into my house.

look like me and Elohim sharing de loom and me not sure what de two of we weaving.

just like de man dress in linen wid gold belt round him waist who appear to Daniel was no man. just like de three fellows wid dutty on dem foot who did come to Abraham was angel hiding demself in three human body.

seem like Angel Gabriel reach Mary gate disguise as a man . . .

"tall and handsome me tell you and shine like smadi take oil rub all over him. and one full head of locks long down to him shoulder. me see him take time and step through de doorway and like how him is a stranger me make my way down to dem yard for me know is only Mary she one into de house."

"and den what?"

"well me hear one big laughing and talking."

"oh! laughing and talking? talking bout what?"

"after me couldn't hear! but him talk and she talk and de two of dem laugh."

"and what after dat?"

"how me must stay in de street and know what after dat?"

"so dat is de whole story?"

"is de time. you don't see? is de time. time is of de essence!"

"how come?"

"dat is four month gone. if is dat man pikni is just now it would show. and don't is just now de bump on Mary belly grow big so we see it and know?"

Jah-Jah have him ways. my wife never sick once. she dancing along like mizmor—a psalm for de harp a song for sweet strings. like dis baby business is moves she making from long time.

one day she approach.

"husband make you and me visit Cousin Liz. if Angel Gabriel wasn't making one big story Cousin Liz on de way wid de promised baby. we can leave de girls wid Pa Joachim and Ma Ann."

so we go.

Cousin Liz baby bump favour a beehive.

"Joe better you stay outside for de start for Cousin Liz maybe feel funny."

"but my love her belly been dere six month now. if she don't hide inside all de time people no must know she insprignant?"

me hang back all de same as Mary greet her cuz.

and me hear Cousin Liz.

"No woman good like you Mary my love and no baby more blessed dan de one in your womb! and who is poor me so make de mother of my Lord come to visit me? for talk truth as me hear you call out and me know say is you de chile in my belly turn one pupalick!"

me never see no woman pretty so!

Mary skin de whole time have a warm steady glow. no mind her belly big her sandal-dem tread de ground easy like prayer. de curl-dem pon her head shift and gleam like de glints in de sharp narrow streams dat cut de hillside.

never mind her pikni precede her like glory she still cooking and cleaning and minding de girls.

when dem romping me caution her.

"mind how you going my beloved. is cargo widout price you carrying dere!"

"Joe me tired to tell you me not no camel nor no donkey and my baby is certainly not no kind of goods. my Babyfather give him a name. if you must refer to de person inside me please call him Yeshua."

den she talk to her belly.

"Jesus? Daddy Joe need to mind him manners. cargo indeed!"

she stick out her tongue and turn back to de girls.

5: Yeshua

me not a disorderly man for tekton cannot work in
confusion.

but order is one ting and orders is a next. in a right world
dem two should align. instruction should be handmaid to
harmony.

such matters different since de Roman downpressor-dem
come. edict turn de domain of intemperate kings. anarchic
tetrarch tink dem run tings over parent and rabbi and high
priest.

so de Roman big boss Caesar Augustus instruct de local
headman-dem to send we back to de town where we ancestor
come from so dem can count we like shekel or slave.

fine me tink. fine. exactly what me need.

Mary looking to have baby any day now. me must take up
myself gather up me and she and go back to Judea from
Galilee so me can register my fambili in Bethlehem where
David people come from seeing as how me is from David
line?

all sake of money?

but me wise now. me know man must live wid what man
cannot change. so me get up dis morning set off down de
road to go look a donkey to make de long journey.

i know in my soul and it worrying me. at de end of dat road is
Jehovah baby.

like me say it have two way to reach Jerusalem. we can travel straight south through Samaria. is a rugged rough route through some hill and gully. not no easy passage for Mary wid her pregnant belly.

but it shorter by two day. sometime maybe three.

is either dat route or a nine-day safari cross de Valley Jazreel den by River Jordan twisting west back again to climb up through de desert to Jerusalem.

at de last of de journey is only one way to go from de holy city to Bethlehem.

now Samaritan do not have no use for Jew. not to say Jew have use for de likes of Samaritan though talk truth me and dem never have no dispute. but what don't happen in de course of a decade can come upon you in one day.

how me could run dat risk wid Mary and Jah baby?

so after we take Judith and Sarah to stay in Sepphoris wid dem grandpa and grandma me going wid my wife and soon-to-be son by gentle Jezreel and de River Jordan.

after we say de Traveller's Prayer we set out early morning.
walk me walk and put Mary pon de donkey.

like how is wet season no day not dawning widout a
rainy promise but today Jah smile on we for sky blue like
cornflower. not a whisper of mist.

we travel some way den we stop and we bite barley bread and
sip Jah-Jah juice.

Jezreel is a wide open basin of dutty—a womb cram wid dark
nourishment. me did tink to cross quick for till now not a
cloud is a cloud but de ass drag him foot though me can't
figure why. Mary belly big but she slight in her body.

we need to put on speed but de own-way donkey take him
sweet time like him out to provoke we. and so him step slow
so him push him foot deeper.

de ting is when it rain Jezreel Valley hold water. if dis foolish
jackass walk in wet de whole day come tomorrow him sick
wid stink foot disease.

me mind sheep and goat but me never tend donkey. is a risk
me can't run.

anyhow donkey ailing travel done!

sky still blue when we eat again bout de sixth hour.

no mind Mary big-belly she quick on her foot. in a flick and a flash she bundle up bread water-skin rug pack dem in bankra basket and hand dem to me.

me take dem from her fix dem pon de donkey.

"Mary we need to consult. need to talk to Jah-Jah. me no tink we can go de long way through Beit She'an and down by River Jordan."

Mary put her two hand pon her tummy and me see it quiver. she look up in my face and she smile.

"why you change your mind Joe?"

i roll my two eye up to heaven come back down.

"de donkey beloved. you see how de ground wet?"

my wife nod.

"if him walk de whole day in dat meke-meke by tonight him hoof sick wid stink foot disease."

my eye make a serious four wid her two. me turn. point up Mt Ebal.

"but like how de road up so rocky and de hill high . . ."

" . . . rain run down de slope so de ground up dere dry?"

my chin answer yes.

"so we best head up dere Joe. Jah-Jah would see de wisdom of dat."

"is a rough route beloved."

"but is de one way to reach so come make we look sharp."

is not just dat de route through Samaria is a punishment
road or dat Samaritan do not love we who come from Galilee.
is also dat dem have some serious tief and some long head
trickster good to take all from de nothing we have.

still best look on de good side like Mary love say.

dis road is de road we forefather-dem set foot on nuff times.
we tread in dem sandal each year when we go to Jerusalem for
de high holy days so is a way me know good.

and no mind it wretched it plenty more short. food and water
will stretch. keep we till we catch Sychar near de Well of Jacob.

de fool-fool donkey take him time up de hill. still no mind is
a climb as him reach dry stony him well happy and step wid a
will.

when me turn and look down de slope of Mt Ebal drifting darkness hug up de green of Jezreel same time ripe sun nuzzling Mt Gilboa to de east. me sniff find a cave. we bed down and rest good. start before heavens wake.

dis route top de ridge is a vexing pathway wid nuff twist and turn up and down and go round come back try a next way for de hill-dem forever remaking demself.

Mary tired. no mind de betrayal of sharp dip and jolt her eyelid-dem close like a long lovers kiss.

when she swaying too far to right or to left me shake her wake her.

"Mary love hold on tight! can't let your backside and de back of de donkey part company until we stop tonight."

we pass Sebaste push on and reach Sychar before dark come down. me make haste fill de skin-dem at Jacob Well den we tuck weself close in de ruins of Schechem.

next day we start early again. de donkey drink deep from a spring on de low mountain slope as we skirt Mt Gerizim and go east to a vale will carry we most of de way to Lebonah. Jahweh cool de hour wid a light brush of wind plus de sky treat we good.

we move smooth through de valley and climb one last hill den sing praise for de town right as evening begin. Mary bearing up but it squeeze my heart when she draw breath and sigh.

we bless bread and eat and recite Maariv and den settle weself into sleep.

me give thanks when we brush off de dust of Samaritan
country and de heavens bless we one more time.

donkey solid on him foot but de ground merciless. look right
and look left and is only rock grow. we walk and kick stone.
climb over climb round and repeat.

bless Jahweh for what leave of Bethel! a old man name Levi
and him wife Abigail have a small kataluma and we stop wid
dem. next morning de old folks send we to de day wid oil
bread and herbs date fig and blessing.

take we almost two day trudging on tough dutty to pass
through Ramah and—praise Jah—catch sight of de holy city!

me was hoping to say a reverent howdy and wave and go long
but Mary look well weary so me make up my mind to try de
next inn.

better outside de city where is not so much scoundrel and
covetous folks. dem will leave we two shekel after dem done
wid we.

next day we don't leave till sun show a faint bloom in a misery heaven. jackass at a clip we pass Jerusalem when me feel some big drop go *plaps* in my head. next ting rain falling so fast and feisty me can't see de donkey side of me. can't spy out a crack to stop and shelter in.

when me see Mary simlāh soak all de way through me tackle Jah-Jah.

El Shaddai is why you do we so?

likl more jackass stumble. me look to one side to steady Mary and discover a dent in de hill. it just fit she me and de donkey. it cold but it dry. me tell Jah-Jah tenky but now simlāh sopping and kethōneth paste on to we frame.

"make a fire Joseph." Mary peel off her simlāh drag mine over my head. "since is wait we must wait we best use de time. dis way de two cloak will dry on de donkey and de tunic will dry on we body."

no mind clothes don't dry good we resume de journey as de cloud-dem oblige.

de last was de worst. wind blow water blind we. box we face. chop we cheek right and left. den snow come. it so cold top and bottom teeth greeting demself de whole time.

my head down looking firm footing fraid for wife and pikni.

"Look Joseph!" Mary say.

and me see David city.

we reach Bethlehem at bout de ninth hour. me make haste
and find Jonathan inn and me knock and call out.

while we waiting i lift my wet wife down from de donkey slip
her arm through my own so she can lean on me.

Mary hand on her belly. de baby low down so me know him
soon ready.

we wait. when me no see nobody no hear not a soul me call
out again. after one long time pass Jonathan first son Amit
push de door.

me clap my hand and lean forward to greet him.

"cousin give thanks! i so glad to see you. dis is Mary my wife."

Amit eye go straight to Mary belly.

"Jah know we well tired. we done nyam but we tired. Mary
have to get rest for she soon born de baby. you can see for
yourself."

like how him eye don't leave Mary middle till now.

de bold face youth tell me him pa sorry but de house choke
up wid fambili come for de census.

likl most me punch him!

when me look back of him me see three mean eye woman
staring at Mary. if bad looks could damage dem would maim
she and Jah pikni.

*but dis not Galilee? susu can't reach so far bout Mary and dis
pikni?*

"de best we can do for de two of you is de animal shed over so."

as him point me turn tail never say no tenky. lead my wife
and de donkey to a bruck down shanty up gainst de hill face.

77

me did figure is me have to bring dis baby.

me did know we not going find no meyaldot in de tumble
and turmoil of census pappyshow. so me make sure to have
salt and wine and nuff oil and me have my knife ready.

me tink back and recall is me did born we last dawta and
help her to life no mind she never stay long. so dis not de first
time.

den me tink and me tremble.

"dis chile here not my pikni. him is Jah-Jah son."

Mary school me always. "find de good in each case!" and is
same so she do.

she look round de cave hole and say "dis can serve Joe. all we
need is a pot to heat water. maybe if you ask your folks at
de inn . . . "

"time you done say Shema me go and reach back wid a pan.
no mind if is beg borrow or steal."

when me bring de pan Mary done take straw from de animal
trough to make broom and clean up de place. she drape de
damp tings de rug green like pasture and de swaddling like
snow on de craggy cave wall.

me quick catch a fire fill de pot wid water and me set down
my knife by de flames.

den me take out my chisel dig two stone from de cave wall
and me shape dem and set dem near where Mary sitting on
de ground two knee wide apart to make space for her belly.

from de birth tide did flow me mix water wid wine put one
side in a jug. as cording to Talmud wine good for woman when
dem making baby. must can help when de pikni on him way.

de babe is Mary first so i know is no rush. when him start
come i will help her to de two birthing stone.

some shouting from over de inn twist my head.

*is what wrong wid my fambili? what manner of confusion dem
making up so? and my wife dat dem scorn bout to bear down to
bring Jah-Jah offspring! fine music to greet Elohim pikni!*

me turn back my head and leap like a lamb when him just
find him foot. likl most my hand-dem wasn't dere to catch
Jesus! Mary bwoy-baby shoot from her womb—a star
shedding de sky.

don't know how but she kneeling on de two stone when him
spill from her body. one full head of hair slim shoulder sturdy
leg and de red singing string.

i grab Jesus. help Mary as she feel for de ground and lie down.
den i pass Jah baby to him ma. she wipe him old man face wid
de cloth me dip in de warm water. clean him eye clean
him ears.

as me wait for de song in de cord to die down me deal wid de
red leaking from Mary womb bleeding gate for Jah son.

i tie off de cord when it quiet. cut it clean. sprinkle salt on de
baby skin and wipe off. den i rub Jesus body all over wid oil.
pass de baby gleaming fingerling to him ma.

Mary swaddle him.

i look on my wife and my wife look on me.

we frighten for de wide open eye of dis just-born baby.

Mary put Jesus on her breast.

him dere sucking lively as him two shiny eye travel over de place—a scrabble of deal board attach to each side of de cave mouth to fashion a shed.

him take in de donkey couple sheep in de corner and three brown sleeping fowl in a roost on de far side rock face.

talk truth is Jesus make me see de poultry for as him eye march me follow de journey.

and i smile and bless Jah for chicken is kashrut and if luck is wid we breakfast for my wife is one fresh boil egg.

Mary feed Jesus and him turn round feed she!

likl more and de two of dem drop fast asleep a hen wid a chick tuck under her wing.

me wonder if Mary going one day set my son to shelter same place.

me well tired from de journey plus my fambili bad treatment burn soul and body. me kiss my teeth. yawn. close my eye.

when me open dem back me hear one crowd outside. me can tell dem is shepherd for sheep smell is a smell i could never forget.

when me go to de space between cave and wall a man of good age tall and grey not a muscle to spare stay right where him is and bow down on two knee as him gaze at Jesus kotch up close to him mother in de crook of de cave.

him touch him head down to de ground.

when she wake see de crowd Mary take Jesus up from de nest of her lap rest him in de manger for make no mistake is him is de draw.

"Joseph please ask de folks to come in."

"we was out in de fields watching over de flock. of a sudden de air turn bright as middle day and we see and don't see de form of a man. was a giant of light come from heaven for surc." so say de old man.

"we well frighten but him say we must not have no fear. today a Saviour is born in de town of David and we must seek a babe wrap in swaddling clothes lying down in a animal trough."

a young fellow step up and him bend him knee too as him reverence Mary and her son. him take up de story.

"den a crowd of angel join wid de first one and dem make up a noise as dem sing an rejoice saying 'glory to Jah in de highest heaven and peace on earth to all who love dem fellow man.'"

"praises to Elohim!" a plump youth give out as him bow on one knee. "we decide since de angel describe how we was to know de Messiah we best look for him."

everybody neck long. some tipping on dem toe. de smallest peep out from de forest of legs.

"dis is my wife Mary. de baby name Yeshua."

dem don't loiter long. de slender old man sweep dem out wid him crook. "dis lamb only now born. him and him ma need shut-eye. make we go tend de lamb-dem we response for."

next day early morning a young woman come wid her bredren. me know dem as fambili for de likeness is strong. dem favour dem pa Jonathan. de girl is de big one and she stop outside. keep her distance. me take notice of dat.

"respect cousin. shalom. i hope you sleep good. i name Martha. is Tobias dem call my bredren back of me carrying de two skin. Ma don't know we come but Pa say to bring food and water."

hear Mary well cheery "morning children. shalom."

"morning ma'am. please de baby born yet?" Tobias craning him neck.

"him born likl while gone. come inside and greet him."

my wife de hostess no mind she just birth pikni.

"him name Jesus" me say proud as puss. "me is him earthly father. him is Jahweh son." as well dem don't hear wid dem head in de animal trough.

"look him smiling!" Martha say.

hear Tobias "true dat but is not all him doing." a shiwee from de manger down on to de ground.

"come Tobias. we best go before Ma miss we."

"please tell your pa nuff thanks and him welcome to visit and your ma and grandma anytime dem ready. we will glad to see dem."

me shake my head hug her when dem gone. "my peacemaker Mary."

"Joe don't you hear what de angel-dem say? my son come to bring peace."

she lean down to change Jesus swaddling.

likl more and Mary and de baby yawning. her two eyelid
flicker and she drop fast asleep wid de babe at her breast.

me take time go over de inn ask Jonathan where me can find
deal board and hammer and nails to patch up de stable so
make likl privacy for my wife and baby.

him say come and him take me inside.

me work fast. me did know never mind me make noise
neither Mary nor Jesus going wake for she beat and him belly
full.

was a lop-sided room wid de chalky cave side for two wall
and a mishmash of wood wid a rickety door for de next.

de minute dem see Jesus is like Jonathan wife and him
mother-in-law was Mary best friend from Jah-Jah create
Adam and Eve. dem send swaddling for Jesus. dem bring table
bench lamp and a next thick warm rug.

come evening dem send bread fish date fig and mish-mish.

Jonathan wife run tings. once Suzanna start smile him send
word we can stay in de inn.

Mary say thanks but no thanks for she and de baby now
custom to de stable wid de animal-dem as company.

eight day pass and is time for de bris.

Jah covenant say is de father must cut de foreskin. me
don't know where to find no mohel in dis town and is me
circumcise my two bwoy pikni.

tekton custom to use pick and chisel and knife so me move
swift and sure.

Jesus bawl but him ma put him on de breast and him suck
hard and quick settle down.

in due time Mary swaddle de baby and we find our way by
jackass to de temple for it too far for Mary to walk carry Jesus.

we present Jah-Jah pikni to de priest say him name Yeshua
and him done circumcise like de law prescribe.

de priest pray "Blessed are You Adonai Ruler-of-Everyting
who sanctify we through de mitzvot and instruct we to bring
we son-dem into de covenant of Abraham we forefather."

Jesus behave like a true son of Jah de whole time.

sun gone down de next evening. Jesus sleeping deep while me and Mary catching a doze.

a rap on de door startle we wide awake.

me get up go look but me cannot believe.

night falling but a ways off for sure me squint out three camel wid three smadi beside. not a doubt dem rich sake of de caravan and de clothes silk and liquid like light on de sea.

when dem walk a cluster of nailhead glisten and gleam and careen at dem waist. close and closer a curving knife shove in each belt stab my chest wid dread. suppose dem arrive to tief way Jah-Jah baby?

"can i be of service?" me put on my dress voice.

a old man wid a beard long far down in him chest hair white as de froth on a Kinneret wave answer me.

"i and my company have come a long way from de east tracking yonder star." him point in de sky to a ball of light. "we come seeking de King of de Jews."

"is who Joe?"

"three great man say dem travel far to see Jah baby."

"well you best make haste bid dem inside from de cold."

dem enter each one wid someting in dem hand.

de old man step stately to study Jesus. him bow down on one knee. de second one favour a man of my age. him walk to de manger and bend down same way. de last youngest one approach Jesus and him fall down flat on him face.

de silence of praise was a grace fill de place.

old man raise him head first. him two hand pleat wid wrinkle shake under de weight of a chest. it well heavy no mind it small—just tefach a handbreadth on each side.

"Casper is my name and gold is my gift to de King of all Kings." him voice tremble as well as him set de chest down.

de man of my age wid a box in him hand is de next one to speak. i work wood so i know. to carve dat all-over design wid scratch awl and bradawl take a whole pregnant year.

my two eye say respect to workman and work.

box smell high of perfume.

"i am Melchior." so de second prince say for me sure dem is prince. "frankincense is my offering to de Lord of all Lords."

de last one is a handsome dark youth. him voice deep but it gentle and low. "i am Balthazar come wid a offering of myrrh for De-Glory-Come-Down-from-de-Stars."

Mary lift Jesus out him cradle and show him off sweet as you please.

"you must hungry and tired if you come from so far. have some bread? oil wid herbs? and some dates or some figs? and you maybe find room in de inn cross de road. we can easy check."

not no maybe—*for certain like how dem so rich. Mary would dress me down if she hear me tinking such a ting.*

Jonathan tell we dem rise before sun straddle day and ride off like dem hear de best news.

when forty day pass it come time for Mary to go up to de temple for de priest to cleanse her.

it no make no sense to me.

it take woman forty Shabbat to make a baby. after dat she must set de chile down in travail and dem have it to say dat is impurity?

so which part not pure? de likl baby? de woman who strive to make de pikni?

but Isaiah declare de ways and de thoughts of Elohim and him prophets is higher dan my ways and my thoughts. so right or wrong me just leave it and do what dem say.

as for Jesus like how him is a firstborn in de tribe of Judah we consecrate him to de service of Jah and offer him to de high priest for a swap. we give five coin of silver to a kohen of de tribe of Levi to release him from de priestly duty El Shaddai require of all first fruits bwoy pikni.

me had was to leave Mary and Jesus in de Court of Woman
and find my way to de Court of Gentiles to purchase two
pigeon to sacrifice to Jah-Jah.

when me come back wid de bird-dem me see a old man wid
Jesus in him hand. Mary stand close by watching as tears run
from him eye gravel down him two cheek to a pit of grey
beard. him fix him eye on Jesus face.

"praises be to Elohim Most High! as of dis day and time
Simeon your servant can go him way in Jah peace. dis baby is
who going save every soul. is him dat Elohim prepare before
all to show Jah majesty to Gentile and Jew and for de glory of
Jah-Jah chosen ones Israel."

after dat him bless de two of we "de parents of dis sacred
chile."

den him hand Jesus back to Mary and insist quiet like him
tears rilling still "is dis chile Jah choose for de fall and de rise
of nuff smadi in Israel and as a sign plenty going to condemn.
him going lay bare de thoughts in de mind of nuff people."

him lip quiver.

"and a sword going to stab your soul too likl queen. in truth
Simeon heart bleeding and bleeding for you."

me don't yet figure out de old man Simeon when a woman
name Anna hair white as chalkstone face dark and dry up
like a date in de sun make her slow way to Mary and me and
Jesus.

Simeon still singing praises as him depart.

seem from long time aback Anna prophesy in de temple. so
dem tell me. she raise face and hand to de sky as she walk up
to us.

"praises to De Most High De-One-Dat-Run-Tings for de gift
of dis chile to redeem all who seek salvation in Jerusalem."
she looking all bout proclaiming dis news and sobbing and
praising same time.

Anna look on Mary. "mother hold him close to your heart
and rejoice in dis moment like how Yeshua stay strong and
smell clean. one day him going grovel in dutty face shove in
donkey doo-doo a fly feast of blood sake of all Israel."

one ting me must say. from me married to Mary excitement reign. not a week pass but we into some pampalam—small row or big ruction.

we did pack up timely to return to Nazareth. as sun set and de new day begin we cross to de inn and render nuff thanks. den we settle down for a good night rest for is home we going home as sky light.

or is so me did tink.

we exit early yes when dark was still riding de wide firmament but is run we did run. to foreign.

not too far after me sleep me dream one angel so bright me look once in him face and den mostly examine him foot.

him talk deep and grave.

"De-One-Dat-Run-Tings send a message for you Joseph son of Jacob. evil man making plan to kill Jah-Jah baby. you and Mary and Yeshua must leave before day stir tomorrow. race like refugee until you reach Egypt. keep out of man way. hide as you go long. disappear when you reach to make sure de chile safe till Jah say to come back."

at de third hour me wake Jonathan to buy a next ass and provision for de journey. give thanks to King Casper we not short of coin.

me beg my bredren send word to Maas Joachim and Miss Ann dat we have to run way to save de baby and we don't know when we coming back.

den we take off like tief as Jah-Jah did instruct heading west to join up wid de Via Maris—de way of de sea.

6: son of Jacob travelling

once we reach into Egypt we don't stay one place.

Mary ask plenty time why we moving and moving. and is true
we punish de two trying jackass from Rafah to Al-Arish to
Farma and Tal Basta.

we sneak into town as de sun yawn and sink and day start.
linger one two Shabbat sneak out well before sun blink him
eye and wake to de world one more time.

when him still likl bit Jesus ride wid him ma but as soon as him
firm on him foot me set him to waddle on de dutty wid me.

me confuse at de first. we go south den turn back to de north
cross de Black River traverse nuff likl stream till we surrender to
a town where we smell de sea strong. me never know why but
once salt rasp my nose my spirit say no. go far de other way.

so we set we sight south pass de great pyramid-dem cross
dc river again pause in three likl town before we rest couple
week in Old Cairo. me must say me well glad Mary make no
complaint bout we lodgings. is lean-to and hut but mostly is
cave like hereso where we kotching.

"my beloved nobody not going look for we in a hole in a hill
in a busy city . . . "

but in truth it well hard. Jesus still suckling. even if Mary
not saying nothing me sure she tired to play like shahaph de
cuckoo and she longing to make her own nest.

after two Shabbat pass in Old Cairo we move on to a next likl
town name Maadi.

one morning before Jesus wake Mary make her protest. she
don't mind de pick up and put down but it not fair to Jesus
for soon as him custom to somewhere we set off again.

me don't have de heart to tell her me discern from de start if
we linger one place too long bush telegram good to take news
to Herod and him not going delay even one day. him will
straight send assassin to kill Jah-Jah pikni.

a next ting me don't tell her for is just now me figure it out.
we traipsing south to get far from de Mare Nostrum since
bossman and dem lackey come and go on dat sea.

you see my dying trial? Mare Nostrum! de Roman-dem tink
dem own everyting down to Jah-Jah water.

when we leave Maadi we cross de Black River again. no mind
him mother say no Jesus trying de whole time to put him likl
hand in de dutty water!

and him love de boat-dem can't finish. some row wid paddle.
some have sail and go wid breeze-blow. some make from
giant reed but de big one dem mostly make out of wood and
sake of de jackass-dem we take de board boat.

it sweet me dat all de boat-dem big or small have a front high
and proud like peacock.

we stop likl bit at Badrashain. after dat we walk on. plenty
more. cross de river to Gabal El-Tair and cross back again
hustling far-far to de south till we come to a place wid low

hill and wide rolling valley.

Mary beg me please if we can ask Jah-Jah to stop now. so she and me pray. when we done we agree Jah approve so we make up we mind for Assiut.

de cave not big but it build sturdy. smadi one time aback make some pillar to hold up de roof. de whole hillside full up of old cave look same way. seem like nuff folks did live here den just vanish one day.

is a curious place but again not so strange. down de hill every morning de folks from around set up market. we glory to find fish and egg. cucumber beans lentils. onion leek and chicory. grain. fig pomegranate grape and date. cow and goat. sheep and lamb.

when me see how Jesus love de lamb dem me start tell him story when him going to sleep bout my shepherding days. me was glad to recall Jacob and Matthan and a time before murderous man.

at de first me surprise when Mary listen to de lore and learn de herding song-dem wid Jesus. den me member she grow in de temple and is not much she know bout life in de world.

me did tink to search round for a cave wid more space but Mary confess she rather we stay where we is like how Jesus make couple friend and dem custom to play likl way down de hill where she can easy see dem. quick reach dem if need be.

so me set my mind to cut one-two tings from de rock all bout. me chop out one table couple stool one bench couple shelf. while me work in de cave Mary learn Jesus and him friend-dem how to cipher and write dem name in de dutty.

me watch Mary wid de three bwoy pikni and me tink of my two and Judith and Sarah. since we leave no day pass we don't commend dem to Jah. beg him cover de brood. hide dem under him plentiful wing.

me did make a fine ting wid Debs in Galilee but how me must weave anyting wid Mary and my son in a cave in foreign?

bout six moon we make life in Assiut.

Jesus strong on him foot now. him frolic de hillside like any goat kid. fetch and carry for Mary. even make couple tings wid my tool-dem. one plate and a bowl. one hilarious spoon.

den one night Jah-Jah send a next angel. him arrive in a dream and talk businesslike.

"Get up Joseph. Jah-Jah want you to take Yeshua and him mother and go back to de land of Israel. it safe seeing like how dem as was trying to kill Jesus now dead."

me was glad talk de truth for dis last likl while de time turn well hot. Jesus play wid him friend-dem inside de cave till dem mother come and take dem home in evening cool. we only go out early morning and when dark coming down and we welcoming de new day.

Mary give thanks to Jah. say dis is de last pack-up till Jesus married!

she Jesus and me set off to reverse de journey.

me did tink Bethlehem would suit we good like how
Jonathan live dere and could help we establish weself.

but pure crosses again!

no sooner we catch Judea me hear Archelaus take over from
him pa and one serious big fraid overtake me.

suppose Herod pikni come after Jah son?

good ting El Shaddai rescue we one more time. a next angel
messenger pay me a visit and say me must try Galilee.

so look like it must be nasty Nazareth again.

time we reach back from Egypt de two likl girls not likl no more. dat tomboy Judith turn a rowdy sixteen and soft-eye Sarah turn a tender thirteen.

we reach Nazareth and couple Shabbat pass. two day into de new week at bout de third hour Maas Joachim visit de yard. him bring date and oil and wine in a new-new wineskin and a frown cut him forehead in two.

Judith just coming back wid her full water jar from de well down de hill for rain done and de cistern now dry. when me first look and see her me heart jump. is Debs very self! she favour her mother can't done.

"Judith my dawta" me say as she step in de yard "say shalom to Grandpa. when you go inside please tell your ma say her papa just reach and him coming inside."

"no please Joe. not yet. you and me need to talk."

so me and him settle down on de bench by de myrtle bush in de back of de yard. him set him staff pon de ground put two hand pon him knee look at me plaintive like.

"Joe me know you just come. me know you well glad to have all your fambili together again. considering all dat me do not quite know how to tell you dis news . . ."

"bout a fellow name Joshua wid a bredren name Luke?"

Maas Joachim smile and him forehead restore. "well for certain me glad you know bout dem two!"

is as well Miss Ann long time research de fambili. widout woman me do not know where man would be!

me glad for de year of betrothal so Jesus could spend likl time wid Judith and Sarah before two of dem leave to live wid Joshua and Luke in dem fambili house.

dat girl Judith set out to try Jesus time and time again. never mind she grow big she provoking same way!

Jesus have a black puss him find and bring home. him Granny Ann take string make a ball and give him. Jesus and de puss love romp in de yard wid de ball.

don't know what come over Judith but she start hide de ball. every place she hide it Jesus straight go and find it like him can smell it out.

so dis day she take de black puss put it up de myrtle tree. de cat like to climb so him find a limb in de sun and him settle down.

next ting Judith go looking for Jesus find him well distressed sitting out in de yard wid de ball in him hand.

"what happen Jesus?" she ask him. "why you looking so sad? is because you can't find de black puss?"

"no. is not dat."

"den is what?"

"is because me have a sister and she hide way my cat and me do not know why. me and she never fuss. me don't do her nothing bad."

is Mary tell me de story for me was at work.

Judith feel so shame she sit beside Jesus take him hand in her hand.

"Jesus my likl bredren . . ."

Jesus give one big grin pick up de ball of string and run right to de tree and summon de cat.

de two girl get married in a big-big wedding. food for so. wine flowing. nuff music and fêting as de groomsman-dem announce de two couple join. we jump and we dance. we sing praises to Jah for Joshua and Judith and Luke and Sarah!

nine moon after Judith make a sweet girl baby. Sarah follow her quick wid two likl twin bwoy.

Mary in her gungo! she weave and she sew and she cook and she bake. she drag me over to Joshua and Luke fambili house any time me not working. she up dere wid Jesus from morning till night.

when de likl girl sick wid three month colic she stay to help Judith mind de pikni.

one evening when her eyelid-dem drooping me venture advice.

"Mary my love you need to take a break."

her two eye fly open wide like patoo. "Joe is three likl pikni into dat one house. Ruth not young like me and four other granpikni in dere already. four plus three make seven."

"exactly one part of my point! you don't want Ruth to feel she old and useless. you don't want to take over her space."

"if you say so Joe. but me do not tink Ruth feel anyting other dan glad for de help."

me don't bother tell her de next part of my point. all de time she and Jesus spend over de grandpikni house is time dem don't spend wid me.

you could say me was just a likl jealous.

*no mind she is Jah babymother Mary still Joseph wife and Jah son
is still Joseph pikni.*

Jesus never shirk work as him grow. not one day. true me is him pa and de shop is my shop but regardless me give him free rein. each morning him set tings in order. den me come and survey shake my head and say "son tings cannot stay so!"

him look on me side-eye. grin. den we set to again and we do it my way.

now and den me hear him hum de herding song-dem me did learn him when him was small. i wonder dose times if de tending of sheep and goat kind might suit my son more dan to craft wood and stone.

all de same we keep on in de shop and him seem like him happy enough.

sometime me and him fuss when tings not in dem right place.

i tell him "Jesus tekton cannot work in confusion!"

him tell me "Pa a bit of commotion stir man invention."

me humph like de old man me is. "till de hammer fall down on your foot bruck your toe? or de chisel chastise your sick thumb?"

dat is a low blow. him poor tumpa sick for him kotch de chisel careless and it drop cut de finger make it bleed and bleed.

but him grow and him see as me dwindle and see.

when de flint of untidy meet de tinder of tidy it kindle de fire in cradle and coffin.

every year we go Jerusalem to keep up Pesach. is a journey take five or six day sometime seven. de whole fambili travel one time. all we kin near and far in Nazareth and Sepphoris come together and form one big caravan.

better so for we take de short way through Samaritan country. like me done say already we no like Samaritan and dem no like we. plus nuff tief and wild animal lurk on de road. so we plenty safer when is plenty of we.

mostly we walk or ride mule or jackass. bag and baggage we carry on donkey cart. pikni love ride de cart-dem. sometime too de old folks when dem foot giving out take a kotch pon de back.

Jesus turn man now so him response for himself. him check wid we now and den as hours beat. sometime him stay wid Judith and Sarah fambili. sometime him wid Miss Ann and Maas Joachim for Pa Jacob and Ma Milcah long since gone to Jah.

Pesach done and we on de way home. everybody eager to reach back to dem yard so we hustling.

like crosses from morning till night one entire day pass and neither me nor him ma don't see Jesus. we don't waste no time. me and she chase from de front to de back of de line.

"anybody see Jesus? we can't find him nowhere."

so we ask so dem shake dem head no. what to do but find we way back to Jerusalem where we just come from?

we turn round same time. we check every inn every tavern

and shop every place we stop. not a sign of Jesus.

Mary she looking worried but me getting vex. someting in my
belly tell me him safe but me can't figure where him could be.
i can't tink what manner of doings could hold him so tight
dat him grieve us wid major worry.

we find him in de temple in Jerusalem.

me and him ma stand one side listening as him discuss wid de teachers compose as you please and answer dem question like him know what him talking about.

him question dem too.

when him see we him end de discourse mannerly and come cross wid a smile.

"Jesus son why you do we like dat? for three whole day your father and me crawl country and city trying to find where you be!"

bwoy don't dip him eye.

"but Ma why you was searching for me? don't you know me big now and me have to take care of my Father affairs?"

Mary look on me hard for she know me rile up. is true him is Jah-Jah pikni but dat surely mean him must observe de mitzvot and de Ten Sayings better dan ordinary smadi?

"son" i tell him "don't do nothing like dis again."

him nod. three of we set out on de way home.

me must not stay my hand because him is Jah pikni. me sure Jah don't mean for me to spoil him one son.

is Matthan my grandfather did first tell me yatush—dem small
flying ting wid de malice of Satan—can make you sick bad.

"you don't sick when it bite not till couple moons pass. first
you cold and you shake. den de fever take you and you burn
like you dead gone to Sheol. you sweat all de juice from your
structure den de body recover and behave like as usual again.
until de next visit."

me sure me and dat wicked insect did buck up in Sepphoris.
de cool time and rain did just start. as darkness come down
mosquito come out like de new day cannot start widout dem.

if is home me was home me would catch up a fire put some
stink grass in it run de small demon-dem. but me was staying
de night wid Miss Ann and Maas Joachim. sometime me
kotch wid dem when me work on de hill. de old folks sleeping
and me don't want wake dem.

so me twist and me slap till me end up wrap round in my
clothes and is only my nose sticking out like a beak. come de
morning my skin was a map of abuse. is why me member so
clear.

and just like Matthan say after bout three moon de sickness
descend. me don't tell nobody all de same. me just cover up
on my mat chill chewing my body and clawing my bones. my
head ache. my muscle-dem ache. me feel to expel everyting in
my belly.

me never want worry Mary or Jesus so after de first night me
move to de workshop. is not anyting strange for nuff times
me live dere when me have a big job and de log-dem stack up
outside. wood scarce in dese parts and me rather don't put

temptation in nobody way. so me stay in de shop till de wood pile use up.

Mary leave food and drink as she usual to do. couple time she try make conversation but me tell her my mind on de job. she must wait till me done.

and me stay and me suffer ten day till it gone.

every time a next father come for a chat Jesus cry excuse find someting him must have to do and depart wid a smile easing round him mouth corner.

all de dawta-dem was a sight to behold. pretty as periwinkle or good wid dem hand and sometime de two combine into one.

for certain worth more dan de bride money me would have to pay.

but Jesus just laugh.

"Pa you must not pay—dem no mind!" and him chuckle at him corny joke.

Jesus give we warning time and again.

"Pa Joe dat young fellow Daniel good enough wid de chisel. don't it? him could give you a hand anyhow me not here. don't is so?"

"son you going off somewhere?"

"Pa me never say dat. me say 'if'. suppose anyting was to happen to me?"

"come now Joe" Mary say. "Jesus make a good point. supposing him was to married? don't you would have to get help?"

so i give it to Jesus.

him never did spring it on us.

sun go down. we three eating quince looking out as a weary today say farewell and a nail prick of light puncture Jah darkling sky.

"Pa and Ma me have someting to tell you."

de way Mary eye shine as she look in him face me know she tinking is a woman Jesus going talk bout.

"Pa not dis Shabbat but right after de next me going leave you and Ma."

"leave we and go where son?"

"me not sure. maybe go up to Antioch. maybe east to Damascus or south down to Egypt."

"but why Jesus?"

"is what me trying to know Pa. is why me must go."

Mary lean gainst my shoulder.

"if him feel him must go Joe we must glad for Jesus. all de same right dis minute we need to retire inside. give yatush plenty space wid dem fast flying wing and dem needle sharp mouth."

i can't figure out how Mary so calm when her son plan to roam only Jah-Jah know where . . .

of course life did go on never mind Jesus gone.

Judith make a next girl den a first bwoy pikni so dat did make three for Joshua and she.

Sarah not so lucky. she carry a next twin. two meyaldot come when she take in but dem couldn't save de pikni. likl most dem did lose Sarah too.

dem declare she need care and further to dat she must not do any work for three moon at de least.

it leave we no choice.

like how Sarah sick is only Ruth and Judith and Naomi and Eva—de two other dawta-in-law in de house—to manage twelve pikni. two for Sarah and Luke. three for Judith and Joshua. three for Noah and Naomi and four for Jude and Eva.

so we talk and decide to ask Simon and Ruth if Mary can stay dere to help mind Sarah.

when Sarah get better my Mary return wid ants in her sandal.

she want start a school.

nobody couldn't stop her. it remind me of how Debs determine her mind Judith was to find her way to de pikni schoolroom wid Zeke and Aaron.

day in and day out Mary at Ruth and Simon house. she learn de pikni to say de Shema. she learn dem de blessing on bread and de blessing on wine de blessing on fruit and de blessing on grain. she learn dem de Ten Sayings and start on de mitzvot.

she learn dem to cook and to sew and to weave. she learn dem to cipher to write and to read.

she learn dem to dance. when Zeke visit wid him wife and pikni him learn dem to sing. everybody join in. Aaron learn dem to play timbrel and clappers and drum when him come wid him fambili from Hebron.

if is egg Mary into de red!

she love de music and dancing de screaming and laughing de whole heap of noise.

as me watch her foot move and her plait swinging free me give it to Jah-Jah.

him make a perfect choice.

when de last likl one stand to recite Torah in de synagogue up on de hill me tell her is time now to stop.

dese last days Mary pining can't stop look for Jesus. she not saying nothing but come early morning me see her stand in de road hand shading her eye chin tilt up and gaze stretching out.

same ting when sun depart at de nine hour cool before night come down and start de new day.

"my beloved you know him don't gone forever. him will show you himself in good time. him own time."

"is not fret me fretting Joe but me miss him. my eye long for de day him fill dem again."

"him will not abandon we Mary my love. and is Adar a good time for us when him leave. me sure you will not see two more pregnant year before him come back."

"me can't wait so long Joe. de next pregnant year is two twelve-moons from now. me can't wait so long."

likl most me never know him!

Jesus brown till him black. him hair long down him back. line criss-cross him forehead and crimp him eye-corner. him cheek-dem suck in. dust cover him hand foot sandal and clothes.

me was not sure it was him defeating de hill one foot den de next. so me shout and inquire.

"who asking if me is me? oh Pa Joe! is you! of course me is me. after me couldn't be nobody else?"

question stand in de air between us for a while as two of we smile.

me run out and hug up de foreign body saying him is my son. feel de grit of de journey. see dutty in him beard in him ears in him hair.

"son you best come inside. best wash off your face and your hand and your foot. your ma going distress if she see you like dat."

"den me better don't preach 'look not to de outward but look to de heart . . .'"

and him grin de mischief him did learn from de tiefing black puss.

three day after Jesus come back de sickness return.

me make up my mind just like de first time not to tell my mellowing spouse two-three streak of silver grooming her hair. when de sky purpling me say how me tired how me certain she dying to talk wid Jesus.

"why you and Jesus don't stay on de porch and chitter and chat for as long as you like?"

me lie down on my mat. first me tremble wid chill. my teeth clatter like clappers. den me fiendish wid fever. my head beating-beating like it going to split and my belly feel like it doing pupalick.

next morning me move to de shop like first time.

"son your gran and your grandpa would love to see you." is so me tell Jesus when him come to find me. "me tink you should visit. spend couple day wid dem. me sure your ma not going mind."

Mary say no she not going mind at all at all.

me stay for a week wrap up in two simlāh and two blanket wid two big water jar standing guard.

Mary come morning time wid bickle for breaking my fast and walk down in de evening wid supper.

"tenky beloved and like a kind soul please set it on de bench. me busy can't done."

me manage till it pass. not a soul de wiser.

109

one forenoon soon after Jesus come back me see him in de
yard wid three youth. me don't like how dem sound. plus dem
stink like dem don't say howdy to water since dem grow big.

me draw him one side. "Jesus is where you find dis lot?"

"Pa dem crufty me know. is three bredren. dem live in a cave
up de hill on de way to Sepphoris. dem ma dead and dem pa
is a wine head long since throw dem out. when me bring dem
in here and bring likl bickle dem nyam like dem never see
food before."

"son why you never take dem to de rabbi? we take care of
we own."

"look on dem Pa. you would go to de rabbi if you did look so?"

and talk truth dem never stay good. like dem scratch in de
dungle for de clothes pon dem back. not a one of de three
have a mouth full of teeth. not a one but him look like hand
foot shoulder jaw bruck one time or a next.

"where dem going spend de night?"

"if you say okay me and dem sleeping in de workshop."

me well glad next day when me don't see no sign of de three.
when me step in de shop me ask Jesus "son where dem now
gone?"

"me help clean dem up Pa. take dem to de rabbi. tell him me
response for de three of dem. him say him will look someting
for dem to do."

de prophet Micah say Jah-Jah insist we do justice and love

136

kindness. all very well but my son have to work. him too have to earn bread by de sweat of him brow. can't be scraping up every stray soul pon de street.

Jesus eye pat de fidgety babe of my soul. "Pa" him say "is okay."

me look on him hard. Jah son but my son too. "Jesus how bout you come wid me to Sepphoris tomorrow to see if dem need a next hand."

Jesus nod and him smile him likl funny smile.

"have to warn you Ma Mary and Pa Joe. de sundown of many new days it will take to recount how far me did travel and what me do and see."

mark you we can discern plenty tings for weself. him hand signify him work for him bread. de grey in him head and him beard tell worries. de line in him forehead say suffering too.

"you member de long time Passover when you find me in de temple and me share dat my Father have business for me to do? de summons to travel and study and learn was part of my Father affairs."

two of we nod we head. "so tell us son. start de story."

Jesus say for de first him go back to de land of him youth. me look on him perplex but him mother she nod.

"to de cave in de hill near Assiut?"

him shake him head no. say is true him set out on de same road to Egypt as we take when we had was to turn refugee. likl most me ask him how him could recall dat but him ma signal me to hold strain.

him reach Farma same like when we flee but him choose de sea spoor after dat. him walk water and sand cross nuff stream and river to Alexandria a city on de Mare Nostrum.

first sight greet him is a structure of a height to behold. on a island near shore limestone and granite climb de sky in a tower.

"but what it is for son? dem make Babel again?"

"no Ma. it have use. on de top is a mirror to catch sun in de day so a boat on de sea far away could know where to sail."

"what bout when it dark son?" for is night when we fish in Lake Kinneret.

"come night time Pa Joe dem make up a fire dat blaze till morning."

it did make me tink back to my fishening days. how a light on de shore tug we in more dan once in a storm.

III

next day we don't hear no more story for de sickness take me again wid a vengeance. me freeze. den me burn. my breath short. me can't sleep. me wake in de night wid my mouth grabbing air. me retch and me retch. when me stand up me stumble for everyting spin.

dis time me can't hide de sickness from Mary.

she say to stop work. she insist me stay home. rest my body.

so me stay in de yard but no mind how me sick each day come like drab hours. is idle not illness make my hand and foot twitch.

when Jesus reach home from Sepphoris me question him bout how work progressing on de stadium. every soul on dat job despise Herod but a body must eat and we know Jah in charge. De-One-Dat-Run-Tings can bend man evil purpose to him almighty will.

patient like a good pa Jesus recite every night de work dat him do in de day.

Mary force me to rest from Shabbat to Shabbat. she tend me like me was a pikni. time de eight day done me sleep sound. me don't shiver. me not hot. me don't puke and me steady like mule pon me foot.

when sun light next morning me set off wid Jesus for de city perch like a bird top de hill.

like how me feel fine Jesus take up him tale.

"is a foreign city but Jah people live dere from a long time ago. it have synagogue pikni school kosher market. me spend plenty day in a building dem call Mouseion dat full up wid book."

Jesus say in de mouse house him study all manner of scroll and him learn bout all manner of tings. him read Torah in Greek and him read it in Hebrew like him custom to.

"all de same de Greek and de Hebrew don't always match. in de Greek Deuteronomy say Moses tell de people 'return to your house'. in Hebrew it say Moses tell dem 'return to your tent.'"

"but how son? how dem change up de Scriptures?

"is not any big change Pa. it mean de same ting. Moses tell dem go back to dem shelter . . ."

me did tink about dat a long time. how a meaning can travel a difference of words like de same tune sound different on flute and psaltery.

Jesus say him study a long time in Alexandria. him stay dere till a angel one night wake him up from him sleep tell him bundle him tings and go quick down de wharf where de ships-dem come in.

till now me can hardly believe what Jesus recount after dat! how him go on a ship for a whole moon of days and a next moon of days till him reach to a place dem call Barygaza.

him come down off de ship and him find himself into a market wid all kind of merchants and goods.

"what kind of goods son?"

"anyting you can dream Pa. frankincense. spices. balm. myrrh and balsam. honey and almonds. linen and silk. peacock and parrot. jewels. silver and gold . . . "

Mary listening quiet all dis time. now she rise.

"time to rest now Joseph. you need sleep. tomorrow sundown when de new day begin Jesus can resurrect de tale of de merchants and marvellous goods . . . "

Mary shoo him and me to we mat. den she blow out de lamp.

me did dream me and Debs and Mary holding on to Judith and Sarah. de sun coming up don't quite light de sky. we was singing and dancing lively up a hill following back of Aaron and Zeke. Aaron playing de harp and Zeke like a hazzan calling de words of de tune.

Jesus wave from de top to say hurry up.

my heart fill my chest and me open my mouth and me sing

bout my life as a garment me weave of fine thread in a myriad colours. Debs and Sarah and Judith and Zeke and Aaron and Jah babymother Mary.

and Jesus.

Jah-Jah son and my son.

talk de truth me well glad it come like it come.

morning light. me was in de shop early for me promise to fix a table for Miss Rachel. is not any big job and me know me could finish before me and Jesus set out for Sepphoris.

me not too long working when me start draw breath hard.

but still anyway my hand firm on de saw two eye measuring de plank of acacia wood long and strong. a fragrant shalom to de morning.

next door to my bench in de grass my pasero slim papa gold finch croon him morning song "boker tov boker tov" wid him yellow black wing and de red round him eye a headscarf of blood.

me was tinking bout Aaron and him music and Zeke in de pikni classroom. me was tinking on how Jesus travel so far to de island of Pharos wid de tower ablaze and sail long on de sea to de great rich bazaar in de east.

hit my brain just like dat. fierce as fire. me did try move my mouth to call out but my mind instruction never reach to my talking string-dem.

den me look for de last.

each ting was itself. me perceive de mind and de meaning of each. every hammer and nail. anvil. awl. water jar. de blue pitcher Jesus make wid him ten teenage finger laying coil upon coil of de white yielding clay. gluepot. goo of glue. grass wid powder of wood. sky deep like a dream. like a story. de place of repose Sheol calling to me.

me member Debs de first time me did see her. spirit loud and proud and de shout of my loins when she and me join. feel de terrors. travail. de babies dat come. de babies we give wrap up warm in we tears to de dust of Adam.

member Debs when she say she don't married to lie down wid no cat and de love we stoke dat very night. member Debs as she dying bequeathing me Judith and Sarah to raise up.

member Mary first time in de temple. her brown like a queen. her green as a meadow. her young as low tide and her old as Ketuvim preserving Solomon Song of Songs.

member how me catch Jesus sliding from Mary womb. plunge my knife in de fire and de wine. slice de cord. de knot what me tie on him belly. son of man son of Jah fill de space betwixt my small finger and thumb.

member how Jesus did love pat de lamb-dem in de market down de hill in Assiut. how me learn him and Mary de old herding tunes as stars button de sky and we rouse a new moon put a old one to sleep.

member Jesus one day de sun in de synagogue blue tzitzit on him garment as him chant Torah. Mary as tears slip down her cheek down her chin down her neck silent stream wetting up her simlāh.

den my son in a trice wid him back bloody up from de slash and de lash of cat o'nine tails as dem tear way him flesh from him bones . . .

and as quick a road wid a light at de end.

new day as sun set.

Notes

Names of God and Jesus

The names of God in this book are many: Father, God, Lord, King of
Kings, Lord of Lords, Spirit of Wisdom, Jah Spirit, Jahweh, Jehovah,
Adonai, Elohim (the name for God used most often in the Old Testa-
ment), El Deah, El Shaddai, Jah, Jah-Jah, Most High, De Most High, De-
One-Dat-Run-Tings, Him-Dat-Know-Everyting, Ruler-of-Everyting,
De-Glory-Come-Down-from-de-Stars. Mary once uses the name Baby-
father. The name Jesus is used at home; the name Yeshua is used by the
angels and whenever Jesus is spoken of formally or in public.

Culture, Lore and Bible Story

Whereas Mary, Jesus's mother, is often present in the gospels, which
served as primary sources for *de book of Mary* (hereafter *dbm*), Joseph
rarely appears. *de book of Joseph* (hereafter *dbj*) does mention Joseph's
paternal ancestors—Jacob, Matthan, Eleazar—according to Matthew's
genealogy of Jesus. I invent a context and life story for Jacob and Mat-
than, who briefly take part in the narrative. I imagine that these ances-
tors of Joseph were traditionally shepherds. Joseph also starts as a shep-
herd, but turns to fishing, finally becoming a carpenter-builder. I'd been
writing for a while when I realized this might explain the shepherding
metaphors Jesus often used. Once Joseph grows up, his story is that of
all Jewish men: he marries in his teens, taking a bride chosen for him,
to whom he is betrothed for a year before she comes to live in his father's
house. However, his first wife, Deborah, and the story of their married
life is of my making. Although *dbj* borrows the idea of Joseph as a wid-
ower from apocryphal writings, as also the legend of how God selects
him to be Mary's husband, in this book, Joseph is a *young* widower. The
Gospels of Matthew and Luke are the sources for Mary's betrothal to
Joseph, his decision to put her aside when he discovers she is pregnant,
and his marriage to her on God's instruction. Non-canonical gospels
(the second-century *Protevangelium of James* or "First Gospel of James"
and the third-century *Evangelium de Nativitate Mariae* or "Gospel of
the Nativity of Mary") provide the story that Ann and Joachim, Mary's
parents, took her to the temple and left her there in service to God. In
response to Old Testament scholars contending that only males would
be given up to service in the temple (as in the case of Eli serving under

146

Samuel), I can only invoke these two non-canonical gospels. *dbj* also follows the (canonical) gospel accounts of the birth of Jesus, the family's flight into Egypt—though not the details of their sojourn—the return to Galilee and subsequent residence in Nazareth, as well as the incident of Jesus remaining in Jerusalem after his parents depart at the end of Passover. After that, Joseph's story in *dbj* is fictional, though the idea of Jesus's far flung travel in the "hidden years" is borrowed from (more recent) lore.

Location

Joseph's local habitation in *dbj* is a Galilean town named Nazareth. Nazareth in the Bible is a mean village, a place so lacking faith that Jesus could perform no miracles. In fact, it *was* small, and though higher above sea level than nearby Sepphoris, could not otherwise compare to that town. Sepphoris, the supposed location of the home of Mary's parents, Ann and Joachim, is an old town, rebuilt by Herod Antipas in the first century. The name Sepphoris comes from the Hebrew *tsipor*, meaning bird, probably because it was perched on top of a hill. It became an important administrative centre with fine buildings, among them, a stadium. Scholars speculate that Joseph and Jesus may have worked on the stadium, since work for carpenters in a small town like Nazareth would not have been enough to keep them occupied.

Journeys

Joseph's first journey would probably have been to Jerusalem with his family to celebrate Passover. As observant Jews, they would have gone every year, very likely via the shorter route south, through Samaria. The longest journey Joseph makes is the marathon flight into Egypt. There are various estimates of the time Jesus, Mary, and Joseph spend in Egypt, from a few months to three and a half years. However long it was, there are up to thirty locations in Egypt, some marked by churches and monasteries, where many people still believe Jesus's family paused as they passed through, or stayed for a time. Their itinerary as described in *dbj* selects from some of those locations.

Geography

Climate, physical features and human settlement in *dbj* are, hopefully, faithful. There are two seasons in the eastern Mediterranean: a warm, dry summer, and a cool, rainy winter. In some winters, it snows. Dews are important providers of water in the dry season. The Valley of Jezreel is a fertile food basket where water gathers in the wet season. Even in modern times, the journey south from Nazareth to Jerusalem is challenging because the hilly terrain is difficult. There are springs on the lower slopes of Mount Gerizim. Cornflowers are among regional flora, goldfinches among the birds, and wild dogs, deer, and antelopes among the fauna. Wood was indeed a rare commodity, and remains so. Fishing on Lake Kinneret (aka Lake Tiberias and the Sea of Galilee) took place at night, and the boats on the Nile were made of reeds or wood. The deserted caves in the hillside around Assiut exist. The men of Israel had many occupations, including those mentioned in this book: farmers, shepherds, fishermen, artisans including carpenter/masons and makers of musical instruments, teachers, rabbis, merchants, doctors, innkeepers, tax collectors, and kings. Women kept house, had and raised children, and did cooking, baking, weaving, sewing, etc, but there is evidence that in the Greco-Roman world of the time, women (working alone or with their husbands) were also shopkeepers, vendors, jewellery makers, fullers, and dyers. Of course, many were midwives.

Jewish language and culture

Inspired by the similar political and linguistic situations of colonized Jamaicans and first-century Jews, I use Jamaican Creole to tell Joseph's story. Hebrew words (e.g., bris milah, meyaldot, mizmor, yatush, kataluma), and names for holy occasions (e.g., Shabbat, Pesach), the Scriptures (e.g., Torah, Ketuvim), and calendar months (e.g., Adar, Nissan), as well as Jewish prayers (e.g., the Shema), represent Jewish culture. Creolized versions of Jewish prayers are a good example of Jamaican-Jewish hybridization. I also embed the story in Jewish belief and practice, so that, *inter alia*, the day starts at sundown; there is a pregnant year, called Shanah Me'uberet, that includes an intercalary month creating two Adars, Adar Aleph and Adar Bet; food is kosher according to kashrut, the Jewish dietary laws; there are prescribed daily prayers and ritual washing; all male children are circumcised; all marriage is arranged in a complex rite involving a bride price, a betrothal lasting for a year, and a wedding ceremony at which the consummation of the marriage takes place, and is proclaimed.

In writing *dbj*, I did give myself some licence. Jesus has a cat, even though Jews did not keep domestic animals. In a region with few trees, where ordinary people have little furniture and often sit on the ground, Uncle Reuben makes a rocking chair. Though most women of the time are illiterate, Mary is not only literate but has broad enough knowledge to teach. I reason that if she grew up in the temple, she probably learned

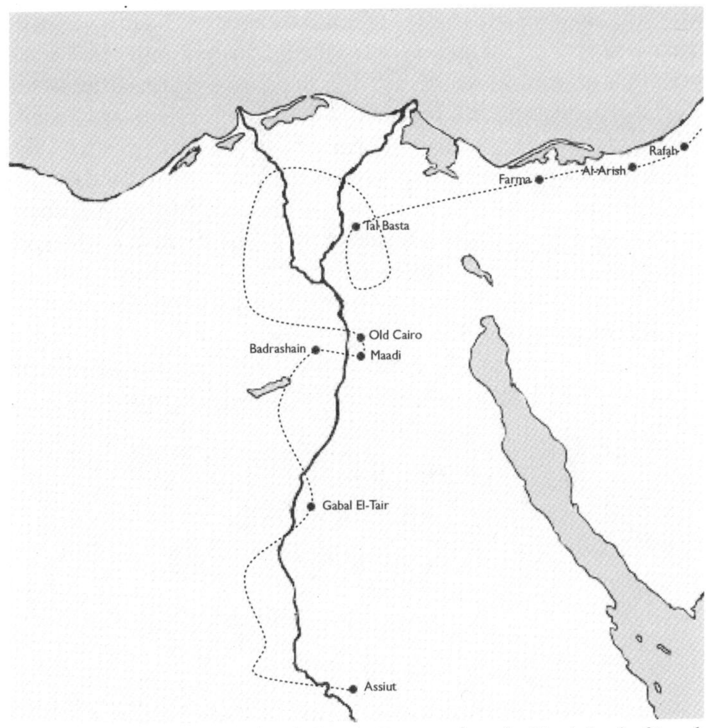

The Flight into Egypt as described in *de book of Joseph*

to read, write, and calculate, and would have known hymns and ritual prayers, as well as the Torah (Law), Nevi'im (Prophets) and Ketuvim (Writings). I thought these would be enough, combined with traditional dances and songs, for a pikni school curriculum.

Jamaican language and orthography

Like *dbm*, *dbj* moves across the Jamaican Creole (hereafter JC) Continuum, being acrolectal or Standard Jamaican English at times, mostly operating in the mesolectal (middle) range, and being almost never basilectal (deep Creole). *dbj* extends its JC usage, however. As in *dbm*, the subject pronouns, *I* and *me* are both used; unlike *dbm*, the English subject pronoun *he* is absent and the JC form *him* is used exclusively. I also attempt to represent the sound of the Creole more aggressively. As in *dbm*, voiced *th* at the beginning of words is always written as *d*, and voiced *th* is also changed to *d* when it occurs at the end of the word

149

with=wid. However, in *dbj* voiced *th* is also changed to *d* when it occurs in the middle of the word *without = widout.* While in *dbm,* unvoiced *th* at the beginning of words is written as *t* only in particularly flavourful words and in emphatic contexts, in *dbj,* unvoiced *th* at the beginning of words is always written as *t,* except in the case of words beginning with *thr* and the word *thanks.* It is also written as *t* in the middle of the words *everyting, anyting,* and *someting.* I chose to use the word *fishening* for *fishing,* not because the word occurs frequently in JC, but because it represents a localized usage that would have occurred in the language of ordinary folks in a small community. As with *dbm,* I missed being able to use the JC plural form of you, *unu.* I chose not to use it because, as a survival of the Igbo word *unu,* it bears no resemblance to any English lexical item and would in all likelihood severely challenge non-JC speakers.

Acknowledgements

I am grateful to the taxpayers of Ontario, who, through the Canada Council, and the Ontario Arts Council Works in Progress and Writers' Reserve/Recommender Grant programs, supported the writing of this book. Big thanks to my late husband, Martin, for being my reader/critic/consultant in a patient and ongoing way over the years, though the illness that preceded his death prevented any input in this book. I am grateful to Marlene Bourdon-King, Jacqueline Briscoe, Dawn Cooke, Carol Duncan, Betty and Donald Wilson and the ON-7 poetry group, and especially JonArno Lawson, Rachel Mordecai, Brian Pearson, Barbara Sheppard, Jennifer Stevenson, Scott-Morgan Straker, and Sarah Tolmie for commenting on the manuscript, in whole or in part, and often saving me from myself. Thanks to Pat Penn Hilden and Timothy Reiss for their continued and unstinting support and encouragement. I remain in debt to my fellow poets and writers and to friends and family, too many to name, for help and good counsel over many years. Finally, many thanks to Nurjehan Aziz and M G Vassanji for taking on board this last-written but first book of the trilogy that I hope grounds and roots the ancient story of Jesus—revolutionary, visionary, son of Man, son of God—by retelling it in Jamaican language. Space does not permit me to enumerate all the websites on which I found material in writing *de book of Joseph*: without the internet, it would not exist, at least not in its present form. *The Lost Books of the Bible*, compiled by William Hone (Konecky and Konecky, 2010; originally published NY: Alpha House, 1926), which contains several non-canonical gospels, was invaluable. Finally, the Holy Spirit, she of the book of Sirach, saved me again and again, in miraculous ways.

Pamela Mordecai writes poetry, fiction and plays. Her collections of poetry are *Journey Poem*, *de Man: a performance poem*, *Certifiable*, *The True Blue of Islands*, *Subversive Sonnets*, *de book of Mary: a performance poem*, *Up Tropic*, and *A Fierce Green Place: new and selected poems*. Her first collection of short fiction, *Pink Icing and Other Stories*, appeared to enthusiastic reviews in 2006, and her first novel, *Red Jacket*, was published in 2015 and shortlisted for the Rogers Writers Trust Fiction Award. Her writing for children is widely collected and well known internationally. *El Numero Uno*, a play for young people, had its world premiere at the Lorraine Kimsa Theatre for Young People in Toronto in 2010 and its Caribbean premiere at the Edna Manley School for the Performing Arts in Kingston, Jamaica, in 2016. Video recordings of her first five books of poetry as well as some children's poems are archived at https://mordecai.citl.mun.ca. She lives in Toronto.